Estado Vegetal

Art after Nature
Giovanni Aloi and Caroline Picard, Series Editors

"Estado Vegetal": Performance and Plant-Thinking
Giovanni Aloi, Editor

Architecture and Objects
Graham Harman

Eco Soma: Pain and Joy in Speculative Performance Encounters
Petra Kuppers

The Lichen Museum
A. Laurie Palmer

Art and Posthumanism: Essays, Encounters, Conversations
Cary Wolfe

Estado Vegetal
Performance and Plant-Thinking
Giovanni Aloi, Editor

University of Minnesota Press
Minneapolis
London

Published by the University of Minnesota Press
111 Third Avenue South, Suite 290
Minneapolis, MN 55401-2520
http://www.upress.umn.edu

ISBN 978-1-5179-1307-6 (hc)
ISBN 978-1-5179-1308-3 (pb)

A Cataloging-in-Publication record for this book is available from the Library of Congress.

Printed in the United States of America on acid-free paper

The University of Minnesota is an equal-opportunity educator and employer.

32 31 30 29 28 27 26 25 24 23   10 9 8 7 6 5 4 3 2 1

Contents

vii **Introduction**
Giovanni Aloi

1 **The Right of the Other**
Interpretation in Four Acts
Michael Marder

15 **Thinking in the World**
Estado Vegetal as Thought-Apparatus
Maaike Bleeker

27 **Theatre as Thinking, Art as Nonknowledge**
Lucy Cotter

45 **Vegetal Mythologies**
Potted Plants and Storymaking
Giovanni Aloi

65 **Attending to "Plantness" in *Estado Vegetal***
Dawn Sanders

79 **"I Can't Move"**
Plants and the Politics of Mobility in *Estado Vegetal*
Catriona Sandilands and Prudence Gibson

97 **Feminist Structures**
Polyphonic Networks
Sibila Sotomayor Van Rysseghem

107 **Soledad**
After *Estado Vegetal*
Mandy-Suzanne Wong

121 **In Conversation**
Manuela Infante and Giovanni Aloi

139 ***Estado Vegetal***
Manuela Infante

159 **Acknowledgments**
161 **Contributors**
165 **Index**

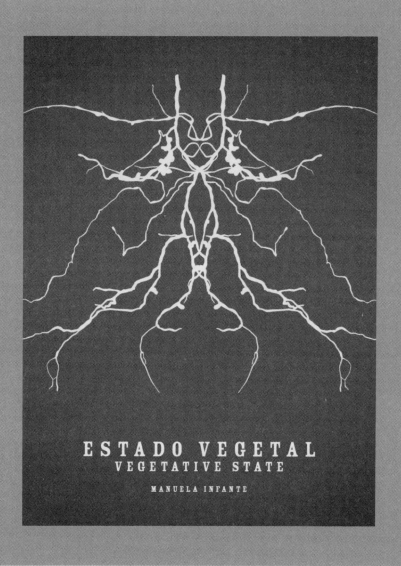

Poster, Manuela Infante and Marcela Salinas,
Estado Vegetal, designed by Javier Pañella, 2017.

Introduction
Giovanni Aloi

It might be its perfect concoction of Pirandellian minimalist realism and Almodovarian absurdist comedy, or the deeply poetic slant underpinning the existential drama it portrays, but there is something powerfully destabilizing about Manuela Infante's *Estado Vegetal.*

Since its first staging in 2016, Infante's riveting piece of experimental performance art has toured the world. From Chile, Singapore, and the United States to Korea, Brazil, Belgium, Switzerland, Germany, France, and Italy, where it was performed to great acclaim at the Venice Biennale 2019, *Estado Vegetal* has quickly collected international awards, received outstanding reviews, and garnered academic praise along the way. Celebrated as the groundbreaking type of performance that reflects the preoccupations of anthropogenic times, *Estado Vegetal* has accomplished what the work of other artists hasn't: it has creatively expanded philosophical thought into a fully fledged artistic expression of nonanthropocentric thinking.

In *Estado Vegetal,* plants are simultaneously form, content, and essence. From beginning to end, the polyvocal monologue acted with impetus and wit by actress Marcela Salinas diffracts identity, displaces anthropocentrism, and uproots our culturally grounded conception of the world in the face of incommensurable trauma and loss.

Permanently connected to the soil and other plants via their roots or ubiquitously fragmented into a multitude of cuttings, grafts, and clones, plants are rarely truly individual beings in a human sense. This inherent plurality of plant life is inscribed in the multiple voices inhabiting Salinas—central is the voice of a mother whose son has entered a permanent and unconscious vegetative state after crashing his motorcycle into a tree. From the mundane to the biblical, multiple identities flicker across the stage, composing a fragmented view of plant–human interactions that transcend space and time.

Ultimately, *Estado Vegetal* casts deep shadows on our hubristic sense of self. How do plants witness, feel, communicate, act, and even reason? What could we learn from their ways of being in the world if we were to overcome the blindness that prevents us from seeing the complexity and intelligence of wholly other life-forms? In this sense, Infante's epic monologue is a vivid and original problematization of the recent critical plant studies philosophies that, from Michael Marder and Robin Wall Kimmerer to Stefano Mancuso and Monica Galliano, have led the new ontological turn in the humanities.

The rise of what is today called critical plant studies began just as the ontological turn in the humanities came of age.[1] Coinciding with the postmodern mistrust for metanarratives and anthropo-centric certitude that, up until the 1970s, defined Western culture, the advent of posthumanism—or at least the prominent popular-ization of it that characterized the 1980s—offered new and valu-able opportunities to relentlessly deconstruct the rhetoric and aesthetics of the brand of humanism that implicitly perpetuated the privilege of the human over the nonhuman and the perspec-tive of the white, male, cis-gendered individual over that of others. At the intersection of human, nonhuman, and technology thus emerged the opportunity to question the very conceptual nature of the human, the elitism of Western philosophy, and its obsolete notions of power and agency. Frantz Fanon and Sylvia Wynter were among the very first to denounce the racist foundations of humanism and its exclusionist approaches to the definition of the human.[2] Thereafter, a host of female thinkers, such as Rosi Braidotti, Karen Barad, Donna Haraway, and N. Katherine Hayles, paved the way for a radical reconsideration of the epistemological foundations in the West.[3] As I have argued elsewhere,[4] the germ of posthuman revolutionary thinking was already detectable in the artworks of Dada and surrealist artists like Baroness Elsa von Freytag-Loringhoven, Marcel Duchamp, Hannah Höch, Claude Cahun, Meret Oppenheim, and René Magritte, to name only a few.

Critical plant studies flourished quickly from these founda-tions. The publication of two issues of *Antennae: The Journal of Nature in Visual Culture* (nos. 17 and 18, 2011) dedicated entirely to plants in art, Matthew Hall's *Plants as Persons* (2011), Michael Marder's book *Plant-Thinking: A Philosophy of Vegetal Life* (2013), Stefano Mancuso and Alessandra Viola's *Brilliant Green* (2015), Monica Gagliano's *Thus Spoke the Plant* (2018), and my *Why Look at Plants? The Botanical Emergence in Contemporary Art* (2018) laid the multidisciplinary foundations of a new and vibrant field of study in which plants always and unquestionably are considered as subjects in their own right.[5]

No longer simply beautiful objects to admire or resources to exploit, in the Anthropocene, plants have plenty to teach us about living on this planet in fuller and more sustainable ways. It is upon this premise that Manuela Infante's *Estado Vegetal* relentlessly unfolds into a deliberately unconventional, yet intensely poetic, invitation to craft new modes of empathy toward otherness—modes that surpass the hierarchies that have thus far impoverished the world around us—and ways of thinking that reach beyond the anthropocentric remits of our sensorial.

A mother's desperate need to empathize with her son's unresponsiveness while in a state of suspended animation triggers important transformative possibilities in the audience. *Estado Vegetal* unfolds around an existentialist desire to fill a communicational abyss, a will to engage with empathic and cultural negotiations that border onto the unthinkable. One of its key objectives is to reconfigure human superiority into a productive vulnerability. This mother's tragedy is our tragedy too—it is simultaneously personal and collective, local and universal: it is the tragedy of being made of flesh and blood and realizing how alienating this can be. "I am an animal. I am novice in the practice of inhabiting, novice in surviving," cries Manuel.

Thou wert all here before I was, nevertheless, it is me who survives with limited understanding, guilty reverse of a mystery, that you understand, however, better than I do. Because you live with time, not against it. I am an animal. My response to the world was to flee, my condemnation, then, was movement. When you stay, I move forward. Where you settle, I evade. Where you settle, I avoid. In the face of difficulty, I avoid. Where you establish, I invade. I am animal.

I hold my head with two hands because in it wallows the question I ask of myself.

Throughout it all, silent and still, witnesses to the unraveling human drama, scene after scene, the potted plants populating the stage appear charged with an uncanny and glowing sense of presence. In the face of our inability to think, and therefore to live beyond the cultural structures that make us human, plants seem imperturbably present and far better than us at life. Through their leaves, branches, and roots runs an incommensurate wisdom that feeds a deeper attunement to the rhythms and essence of a world we think we own but that, in truth, relentlessly eludes us.

This volume is not a classical analytical dissection of a performance but a companion in which scholars, authors, and artists whose work has focused on performance studies and/or the recent emergence of plants in contemporary art and philosophy creatively engage with the specific challenges that *Estado Vegetal* poses. Thinking about, with, and through plants today requires the crafting of new approaches to writing that surpass the boundaries of classical academic formats. It is in this spirit that the book features a broad range of genres and approaches that also include experimental poetry and fiction. Each author focuses on a specific aspect of the performance to outline sets of ramifications and rhizomes—invaluable opportunities to think with plants through art beyond the structural limitations of Western thinking. The purpose of this book is, therefore, to expand, magnify, and reconfigure the original text coauthored by Manuela Infante and Marcela Salinas through a strenuous process grounded in improvisation, to tease to the surface important subtexts or reflect on the cultural frameworks that have relentlessly objectified plants. The result is a rich and often unpredictable, multidisciplinary set of perspectives. Each contribution is an opportunity to think with and beyond the performance from the stage to the reality of human-plant relations in which we daily engage. Featuring the transcript of a conversation I had with Manuela Infante in 2019, as *Estado Vegetal* took to the stage at the Museum of Contemporary Art in Chicago, as well as the play script, this book provides a timely and important contribution to the critical plant studies output thus far.

At a time in which the effects of climate change urgently demand us to reconsider our fraught relationship with the planet, *Estado Vegetal* reminds us that our corrective actions must be grounded and guided not solely by our interest in the future of this planet but by a genuine reappraisal of our ethical and affective bonds with plants.

Notes

1. For an overview of the ontological turn in the humanities, see Paolo Heywood, "Anthropology and What There Is: Reflections on 'Ontology,'" *Cambridge Journal of Anthropology* 30, no. 1 (2012): 143–51; Heywood, "The Ontological Turn," in *Cambridge Encyclopedia of Anthropology* (Cambridge: Cambridge University Press, 2017); Eduardo Kohn, "Anthropology of Ontologies," *Annual Review of Anthropology* 44, no. 1 (2015): 311–27, https://doi.org/10.1146/annurev-anthro-102214-014127; and Eduardo Viveiros de Castro, "Zeno and the Art of Anthropology: Of Lies, Beliefs, Paradoxes, and Other Truths," *Common Knowledge* 17, no. 1 (2011): 128–45.

2. Frantz Fanon, *The Wretched of the Earth* (New York: Grove Press, 1968); Sylvia Wynter, "Unsettling the Coloniality of Being/Power/Truth/Freedom: Towards the Human, after Man, Its Overrepresentation—an Argument," *New Centennial Review* 3, no. 3 (2003): 257–337.

3. Rosi Braidotti, *The Posthuman* (Cambridge: Polity, 2013); Karen Barad, *Meeting the Universe Halfway: Physics and the Entanglement of Matter and Meaning* (Durham, N.C.: Duke University Press, 2007); Donna Haraway, *Simians, Cyborgs, and Women: The Reinvention of Nature* (New York: Routledge, 1990); N. Katherine Hayles, "Unfinished Work: From Cyborg to Cognisphere," *Theory, Culture, and Society* 23, no. 7–8 (2006): 159–66.

4. Giovanni Aloi, "Registering Interconnectedness," *Antennae,* no. 37 (Autumn 2016): 5–22, and Aloi, "The Milk of Dreams: A Posthuman Revolution at the 59th Venice Biennale," *Flash Art* 55, no. 339 (2022): 34–30.

5. Giovanni Aloi, ed., "Why Look at Plants?," special issue, *Antennae: The Journal of Nature in Visual Culture,* no. 17 (2011); Aloi, ed., "Beyond Morphology," special issue, *Antennae: The Journal of Nature in Visual Culture,* no. 18 (2011); Michael Marder, *Plant-Thinking: A Philosophy of Vegetal Life* (New York: Columbia University Press, 2013); Matthew Hall, *Plants as Persons: A Philosophical Botany* (Albany: SUNY Press, 2011); Monica Gagliano, *Thus Spoke the Plant: A Remarkable Journey of Groundbreaking Scientific Discoveries and Personal Encounters with Plants* (London: Penguin, 2018); Stefano Mancuso and Alessandra Viola, *Brilliant Green: The Surprising History and Science of Plant Intelligence* (Washington, D.C.: Island Press, 2015); Giovanni Aloi, ed. and principal au., *Why Look at Plants? The Botanical Emergence in Contemporary Art* (Leiden, Netherlands: Brill, 2018).

Manuela Infante and Marcela Salinas, *Estado
Vegetal,* 2019. Photograph by Maida Carvallo.
Copyright Manuela Infante.

The Right of the Other
Interpretation in Four Acts
Michael Marder

Prologue

The mis-en-scène of interpretation is wanting—its lighting too harsh, its set predictable, its props banal. All too often, interpreters are convinced that they elaborate directly on the materials within their critical purview, forgetting that their engagement is unfolding on a stage of sorts, the stage they prepare and keep constructing throughout their acts of interpretation. That is why their accoutrements are so sparse and rudimentary: they do not suspect that they operate with any.

Deconstruction has done a great deal to draw attention to interpretation's mis-en-scène. But disproportionate scrutiny of what we are actually doing when we do something can be as detrimental to interpretative action as taking its context (and, indeed, its staging) for granted. If one is not careful, one might be left with the set, the props, the possibility of staging, an empty stage, and nothing else. For its part, self-scrutiny runs the risk of deteriorating to narcissistic navel-gazing, camouflaged as criticism.

The art of interpretation must, therefore, navigate between the Scylla of an immediate confrontation with the interpreted and the Charybdis of mediations and mediations of mediations. This art is all the more indispensable when it comes to Manuela Infante's *Estado Vegetal*. The Scylla of a non-self-conscious critical elaboration would do precisely what *Estado Vegetal* vehemently refuses, namely, talk *about* plants and their staging, rather than letting the staging and the plants speak *for* themselves. The Charybdis of intemperate mediation would put critique in the spotlight, similarly stolen from plants. A negotiation between the vegetal text and its context (in which we might participate; of which we might be but a tiny part) has to be ongoing and open-ended. The art it entails is the adeptness of shifting between the context and the text without prioritizing either of these elements.

What, brushing upon the age-old question of truth, Infante teaches us is that the right to interpretation is the right to be claimed not by the interpreter but by the other. On one hand, we could consider anthropocentrically inflected human worldviews, the play, and the hermeneutical exercise as so many prisms, or superimposed lenses, distorting the truth of plants. On the other hand, in light of a revised notion of interpretation as the right of the other (including, first and foremost, the vegetal other but also the artistic endeavor revolving around plants), the prisms and the lenses turn out to be areas of the other's skin, or, speaking generally, of the living-breathing surface of appearances that—vegetal or human, animal or "inanimate"—both present themselves and are presented to the senses. The question, then, is how to put interpretation to work, how to put it onstage, while preserving its right, its luminosity and veracity irreducible to the metaphysical notion of truth.

Act 1: Event

It would be fair to say that *Estado Vegetal* is a unique event in the world of contemporary theatre. Here is, finally, a play that stages plants neither as background materials nor as anthropomorphic projections onto bits of natural environment. In a certain sense—thanks to the ventriloquizing mediations of Marcela Salinas, the dramaturgy, and the script—the plants themselves are actors, active agents in theatre, in life, and in the *theatre of life* to which this work of art alludes.

A landmark production, *Estado Vegetal* gives us plenty to think with regard to the event of vegetality. Unfolding in a gap between the speeds of plant movement and technologically enhanced human mobility, the play imagines different possibilities for an encounter of these strikingly mismatched temporalities. We can fruitfully discuss such possibilities under the heading of the *event*, which is how I interpret Raúl's assertion, applicable as much to a tragic accident as to vegetal growth: "This is a coming that cannot be seen."

The event arrives unexpectedly. It is always a surprise, even if it has been long in coming. A coming that, on the contrary, *can* be seen is not an event but the present modality of time. Expressed in the drily economistic language of modernity, the end product erases the scaffolding of the processes that have culminated in it. The first (and pivotal at that!) coming that cannot be seen in an eventful encounter with plants in *Estado Vegetal* is Manuel's motorcycle accident. As he runs into a tree at full speed, the motorcyclist traumatically bridges the gap between vegetal and human temporalities—in the physical, psychological, and onto-logical senses of trauma. Another unseen, or unforeseen, coming is Nora planting herself, half-buried, in the ground underneath the floorboards of her house. Upon delivering her body and dwell-ing to plant life, she, too, surmounts the divide between human and vegetal paces and rhythms of existence, though this time much more softly and consciously, if, by no means, less shockingly.

The unseen coming of the event meddles with the string of moments we call time either by abruptly cutting its thread or by stretching time out indefinitely, until it abuts space. Its modali-ties correspond, nonetheless, to the phases of plant time: sexual reproduction and vegetative growth, letting the seed drop (or pol-len fly) and extending branches (and multiplying leaves). These modalities are the thresholds of human time-consciousness, be-yond, below, or above which we are unable to accompany develop-ment, or lack thereof, any further.

Manuel and Nora earn the right to interpretation insofar as they are each on their path to becoming-other, to becoming-plant, which means, above all, to living and dying otherwise. They personify vying hermeneutical approaches to the event of the human–plant encounter. The first stands for a coming that can-not be seen because it is too fast, the distance collapsing suddenly when we crash into the very thing from which we are alienated, in a head-on collision with that which we thought we had escaped. The second is a coming that cannot be seen because it is too slow for human perception to register: a gradual merging with, grow-ing in, and getting absorbed into the earth and the vegetation that covers it at a tempo that approximates that of the plants, "living within time, not against it." Despite a marked divergence in approaches to the event of the encounter, the message is that, whether or not we choose it, humanity ends up in a situation of being unable to sustain its alienation from vegetal life, which either violently intrudes upon or steadily reclaims us to itself.

The accident's prehistory (assuming that this word is appropriate) blends the two senses of the event. Overhanging power lines, a tree branch ends up touching electrical cables and causes an accident before the accident, the blackout, during which Manuel on his motorcycle hits a tree. The "unrestrained," "excessive" growth of the branch, as Raúl characterizes it, is the event of growth that is there for everyone to see and that is, at the same time, nearly invisible, unseen, and, by implication, unforeseeable: "Of course, we could say that it was just a matter of looking up and one would have been able to see it coming, but the thing is, you don't see a tree move."

The eventful prehistory of the accident is suspended between an indefinitely long period when nothing at all seems to happen and a happening that strikes in a literal flash. On one side of this abyss, the growth of a branch does not present itself to our sensory and cognitive apparatuses in the shape of a process. Whereas the branch appears in plain sight, its growth disappears, either due to our presumption that plants live in a state of torpor or due to the irreconcilable paces and rhythms of human and vegetal ontologies, responsible in part for this presumption. On the other side of the abyss, in a blinding instant, the branch touches power lines, becomes engulfed in flames, and causes a short circuit. On both sides, the process is erased: here, because the process of growth is too slow to detect; there, because the flash is too fast and intense to stretch out into a sequence of distinct steps. It is between these contrasting ways of doing away with the process—in the abyss—that the event flourishes. And it is a fall (or a rise) into this abyss that gives the impression of having bridged the gap between human and plant times.

Act 2: State

Estado Vegetal: already this expression, doubling as the play's title, invites unrelenting reflection.

Estado Vegetal is used to designate the condition of a human being whose vital functions have been drastically diminished to the bare minimum of breathing, autonomic and motor reflexes, and sleep-wake cycles. This is the sense in which Manuel's mother laments her son's fate, asking, "And what do I do with a son in a vegetative state? Do I water him?! What do I do? If he can't move, he can't move. How does something that can't move live?"

The adjective *vegetative* jumps out at us on account of how it unjustly attributes passivity and immobility to plants. These qualities are subsequently transposed back onto a human who, for one reason or another, has little or no conscious awareness. "To vegetate" is taken to mean "to idle," "to avoid exerting physical or mental efforts," even if, recalling the Latin etymological connections to vigor, the verb also betokens the exuberant growth and proliferation of plants. What goes relatively unnoticed next to *vegetative* is the noun *state,* with its multilayered set of significations.

In a highly selective determination of its meaning, *state* connotes for us something stable but also static and stagnant. The word *stasis,* from which our *state* derives, effectively implies all of these things and also points in the exact opposite direction of strife, all the way to a civil war. Just as *vegetation* condenses and holds in its semantic reserves the bustling activity associated with vigor and the sheer passivity of idling, so, at its origins in *stasis,* state combines rest and unrest, persisting in peace *and* at war. These words carry a speculative charge in the strictly Hegelian sense of speculation that, all at once, posits and negates a given meaning. In *vegetative state,* the charge is redoubled, as each of its two components says and unsays itself in a powerful contradiction affecting our comprehension of movement.

On the passive, peaceful, or pacified side of *vegetative* and *state* alike, movement appears to be absent. Hence the mother's words "If he can't move, he can't move. How does something that can't move live?" But, as we now know, immobility is only half of the semantic story told by speculatively charged words. Vegetative growth is extensive movement without dislocation, the expanding journey of a plant along with, rather than against, the place it occupies. The state is intensive movement, similarly exempt from the demand to leave the locale where it is. (I note in passing that a political state bent on moving extensively, on growing past its frontiers, is no longer a state but an empire.) Manuel's mother is formally correct: according to the ancient association of movement with life, that which does not move also does not live. Intensive and extensive types of movement are, nevertheless, possible without changing one's place, which, in turn, changes with the one *in* it. The assertions "a plant lives" or "my son in a vegetative state lives" do not sever but perhaps strengthen the conceptual ties between *kinesis* and *bios*.

The complex event that is the motorcycle accident is thus a point at which, rather than the mobile hitting the static, different trajectories of movement intersect. It is what transpires when the ever-accelerating, self-dislocating movement from place to place collides with vigorous movement in a place. Curiously, Manuel's mother acknowledges the tree's own vigor (its subjectivity, we might say) when she proclaims that "the tree is the culprit." To be culpable is, after all, to be a subject capable of having acted otherwise. With this proclamation, she obliquely recognizes that those involved in the collision were not a moving actor and a thing at rest but actors moving in their different ways. Thereafter, she buttresses this recognition with a quasi-political depiction of the tree's action.

Speaking of "a quasi-political depiction," I have in mind the closing lines of the play: "The tree brought him to his kingdom. . . . In that moment, in the dark, they took my son away to another kingdom. That's what they're plotting. Someone has to stand in the other's shoes. I understand." He, Manuel, is the grammatical, logical, and ontological object of the tree, who transports him to "another kingdom"—an essentially ambiguous expression that may be read either in a political or in a biological key, or, again, in line with the political subtext of the biological system of classifications. Epistemological and political, the state changes (it moves, since change or metamorphosis is yet another type of movement), and the culprit for Manuel's change of state, for causing him to transgress the borders of *his* kingdom, is a plant, the tree. That a state static in itself, standing in and by itself, may and does become another state hints at the fact that its innermost possibility is in being deposed or, at least, repositioned. The stance of the state (human, vegetal or vegetative, or of another kind altogether) is a temporary position, at the mercy of the vicissitudes of time,

defined by the ephemera of the shifting context and circumstances. "Someone has to stand in the other's shoes"—even if those
shoes turn out to be roots—and, so standing, abandon the identity of some *one* while falling short of identifying with the other.
Manuel: "To be oneself, to be just one self, is a seasonal event." Is
this what, at the edges of understanding, his mother understands,
as her last words in *Estado Vegetal* suggest?

Act 3: Life

On to act 3, then! But is this just one act among many? Or the ac-
tuality of every act on the stage or stages of the *theatre of life*? It
is impossible to think life seriously unless silent consent is given
to the theme's overflow past its ideational confines. Life is excessive; it is an excess—if not the excess—the excessiveness of every
going-outside-oneself. Plants embody this quality of life exceptionally well, as Raúl confirms in his attempted explanation of
the accident. They are the lead actors in the theatre of life and
the infrastructure of that theatre, exceeding the tripartite distinction between the staging, the staged, and the stage on which
action unfolds.

The notion of life predicated on the movement of going-out-
and-beyond-oneself wreaks havoc in the colloquial views of life
and death. Metaphysics and theology tend to frame the soul's
existence after death in the otherworldly *beyond,* whereas life is
thought of as total immersion in immanence. But what is death
against the backdrop of life's excessiveness? How does death
exceed that excess? Is it beyond the beyond of vitality, or—and
this might amount to the same thing—is it the stricture of self-
identity, whereby one no longer or not yet goes outside oneself?
Moreover, if the vegetative state is a gray area between being alive
and being dead, then it is suspended between going beyond and
making not a step beyond. Whatever stirs in it moves without
moving forward.

Insulting as it is to the exuberance of plant life, the clinical
term *vegetative state* inadvertently gets something right about
the relation of this kind of vitality to death, namely, its non-
exclusivity. Manuel proclaims in his ardent monologue, "May

death be something that occurs in my chest, while my back, in turn, is born, so I never get the absurd idea that we are moving forward." The events of life and death, of being born and dying, take place in different parts of the vegetal body simultaneously, frustrating our usual expectation that an organism emerges and perishes all at once and as a whole: here in this moment, not-here (yonder or nowhere) the next. To harbor such an expectation, we must, first, associate death with the beyond and, second, integrate a living entity into a totality, which biologists call organismic. Yet, it is life that is never entirely here, not death, and vegetal life, for its part, defies every act of gathering into a whole. Without leaving the place of its growth, plant is both here and there, dead and alive; a human, ruled by "the absurd idea that we are moving forward," is neither here nor there, neither dead nor alive. This does not prevent some of us from fantasizing about another fate that would be in store for the human, seeing that vegetal life is not reserved for plants alone (as neuroscientists Bryan Jennett and Fred Plum, who coined *vegetative state* in the footsteps of Xavier Bichat and Walter Timme, must have also perversely realized).

Organismic death, then, implies the finality of ceasing to exist. Measured by this yardstick, plants do not die, and the mother's question—"But if you never die, then how can we say you're alive?"—logically follows. On the stage, where plants are barred from the spheres of the living and the dead, a masquerade continues: plants and humans exchange places, or, better, they exchange excessive ties to a place (which is not the same as heedless immersion in the *here*) for sheer placelessness. Lacking secure attachments to a place, humans entrust life and death to time, to a successive, if unrepeatable, series life-death separated by the absolute cut of transcendence. The simultaneity of vegetal life and death renders these occurrences space-dependent, contingent on and influencing the place in and with which a plant grows and rots, the place that it exceeds and that exceeds its own bounds thanks to vegetal movement. Conditional *if . . . then* clauses no longer apply because they require a time lag, however infinitesimal, between their conditioning and conditioned portions. In a clear violation of the rules of formal logic, a plant dies *and* lives at one and the same time.

Act 4: Understanding

Where does understanding stand with respect to the event and life? Does it not stand *under* them, unable to gauge their immensity by those bits that are available to it? Is this standing-under not its own vegetative state, indicative of how understanding itself hovers between life and death, with minimal vital functions allowing its apparatus to survive?

We've already read or heard the words of Manuel's mother, closing the play: "I understand." Devoid of an object, her understanding is mysterious, to say the least; it borders on a mystery also because what precedes its affirmation is the injunction to "stand in the other's shoes." Unbearably full, understanding grows impenetrable, dense and thick. In these conditions, it is highly questionable whether the goal is to understand the other, especially when the event and life itself are at stake; to understand oneself following the Delphic injunction "know thyself"; or to understand the other as oneself and oneself as the other.

Several voices in *Estado Vegetal* express their anxiety and their desire for understanding the other and for being understood. Raúl on unrestrained plant growth: "Do you understand me?" In this context, he offers the analogy of a growing city that extends in every direction, so as to "establish some sort of paragon for your better understanding." The same character gives, also for the sake of improved understanding, the example of an excessive reaction to this excessive vegetal growth, namely, "severe pruning," which means "leaving it [the tree] so to say as amputated." Nora, speaking to plants, inquires, "What do you mean I am not understanding your problem . . . of space"? While Joselino gives testimony of the accident, musing about the "slow coming" of plants and the obscurity of their intentions, he keeps asking, "Do you understand me?" and adds, "It's written in the poem left by the lady; I brought the paper so you can understand." "But do you understand that I now have a son in a . . . in a vegetative state?" is the heart-wrenching question Manuel's mother poses in a prelude to her profession of understanding.

It is as though one could cobble up a miniature play within the play by putting together a compilation of the uncertainties, worries, and glitches of understanding not only mentioned by the characters but also implied in sudden transitions between different voices and times, let alone in attempts to communicate with plants. But, although these concerns are necessary—unavoidable, even—they are misplaced. Infante with her human and vegetal cast does not, in the end, aim for understanding. Nor is it understanding that my plant-thinking strives to foster, particularly on the traditional grounds honed by Kant, who construes it less as a psychological process and more as a cognitive structure comprising empty molds to be filled by data drawn from experience. *Estado Vegetal* and plant-thinking elude such a model of understanding to the extent that they are interested in being with plants and, at the limit, being *as* plants, while maintaining the infinite distance that makes plants other and so incongruent with any preexisting molds.

What remains of understanding when interpretation is the right of the other? Is there not a very real possibility that I would be understood without myself understanding much, if anything, about the other or about myself? Preoccupied with the idea of seamless communication, "Do you understand me?" hides a more basic question bereft of a definite response: "Do I understand myself?" "I understand," says Manuel's mother, neglecting, for obvious (I would say *understandable*) reasons, to specify the object of understanding, be it as intimate as herself.

Manuel is more precise than his mother. Addressing plants in the midst of what one assumes to be his vegetative state, he observes, "Thou wert all here before I was, nevertheless, it is me who survives with limited understanding, guilty reverse of a mystery that you understand, however, better than I do." He links understanding to life and longevity as much as to survival, to the afterlife, to a vital process that should have ended but did not. Inscribing it in time (a sequence or a succession), Manuel performs what he is talking about, exhibiting the "limited understanding" of a survivor who forgets that the life-death of plants is closer to a spatial relation of simultaneity than to a temporal chain. And yet, he remembers his forgetting—a remembrance that situates him on "the guilty reverse of a mystery" we have been tracking all along. Which mystery? Succinctly and somewhat enigmatically put, it is that of interpretation as the right of the other.

Epilogue

Before drawing the curtain on these four acts, I cannot fail to notice that, in them or through them, I have tried to put the right of the other to work. A right is a mere possibility, a codified, legally stipulated entitlement. It is purely theoretical, unless the rightholder exercises it. Furthermore, colored by liberal and neoliberal ideologies, rights become statutes that, in a wholly formal manner, *create* the legal subject and, on the obverse of this creation, expose everyone who and everything that has no rights to unlimited violence and appropriation.

If the mis-en-scène of my four acts amounts to an argument, it does not advance the claim that plants, like humans, should have a right to interpret the world, that is, that this unspoken "human right" (denied to many human beings, to wit) should simply be extended to plants. Valuable as such a theoretical move might have been, it would have done no more than analogize plants to ourselves, their time, modes of being, life, and understanding comprehensible with reference, and in comparison, to our own. *Vegetative state* (and Infante's *Estado Vegetal*) invalidate such well-meaning, albeit insufficient endeavors: breaking the analogical structure twice, they show how the other is within us and entirely different from "us," who are, thereby, different from "ourselves."

The right of the other belongs to another flesh-and-blood human, not to an abstract prototype of humanity, and to the other-than-human, reversing the conventional movement of analogy. This right, which extends to the human as to a creature inhabited by *and* living at a distance from its other, is the right to interpretation. Rather than the right to be interpreted, it is the right to interpret, which does not commence with me. I may only hope to be under its sway after the fact, tentatively, because, far from the place of authority and of the author, my position (my *state,* if you will) is forever derivative and incomplete: hence, survival with limited understanding.

Interpretation accompanies, shadow-like, every intention to act upon and exercise a right. In the middle between theoretical and practical impulses, it is, in itself, an art. As the right of the vegetal or vegetative other, it is actualized in critically and existentially parsing out the time-space, ways of being, life-death, and understanding *of* plants—stemming from plants, pertaining to them, and affecting us, too, at the limits, far from outwardly delimiting our proper form, traversing us on the inside. The truth of interpretation has nothing to do with an externally postulated standard of veracity; it is the effect of the genitive (of the *of*), which holds all the overdetermined clues to the riddle of right.

Note

This chapter benefited from the contribution of the Basque University System research group IT1469-22, "Social Change, Emerging Forms of Subjectivity and Identity in Contemporary Societies."

Manuela Infante and Marcela Salinas, *Estado Vegetal,* 2019. Photograph by Isabel Ortiz. Copyright Manuela Infante.

Thinking in the World
Estado Vegetal as Thought-Apparatus
Maaike Bleeker

In a succession of associatively connected scenes, *Estado Vegetal* reflects on differences between human modes of perceiving and sense making and those of plants. A recurring motive in the performance is the relationships between human and plant respective outlooks on life, the nature of their embodiment, and how these modes of embodiment put them in radically different positions with regard to movement, time, representation, and self. *Estado Vegetal* presents what might be called a new materialist reflection on what Donna Haraway describes as the *situatedness* of practices of relating to the world and of making sense.[1] How the world comes to be known is a correlate of the (organic and inorganic) bodies involved in perceiving and understanding and their social, cultural, technical, and other specificities. The anatomy of humans and plants affords different ways of coupling with the world and different ways of participating in larger *apparatuses* in and through which the world becomes meaningful. Through a playful confrontation of human modes of thinking with what might be the logic of plant thinking, *Estado Vegetal* takes the audience through an exploration of a less human-centered perspective on the world, as well as a less human-centered consideration of practices of making sense and thinking. In so doing, *Estado Vegetal* demonstrates the potential of what I propose to call *thought-apparatus* in theatre: an expressive modality that engages audiences in a mode of thinking that happens in the world rather than solely in the mind of the autonomous human subject, therefore conceiving thinking as a sensuous and sensory practice in which mind and body become indistinguishable. This understanding of theatre as thought-apparatus draws inspiration from Karen Barad's notion of the apparatus in combination with, on one hand, the idea of the thought-image as foregrounded by Walter Benjamin, Theodor Adorno, and other European writers in the 1930s and 1940s and, on the other hand, a nonrepresentational understanding of thinking as a creative practice of confronting chaos by making connections, grasping relations, and composing form, as proposed by Deleuze and Guattari in their *What Is Philosophy?*[2]

The thought-images of historical writers, Gerhard Richter argues, may be understood as "conceptual engagements with the aesthetic and aesthetic engagements with the conceptual, hovering between philosophical critique and aesthetic production."[3] Similarly, the thinking that produced and is evoked by *Estado Vegetal* crosses over between the conceptual thinking of philosophy and the thinking through composition of art. *Estado Vegetal* as thought-apparatus engages spectators in speculations about plant thinking in four different meanings of the term identified by Michael Marder, namely, as referring to (1) the noncognitive, nonideational, and nonimagistic mode of thinking proper to plants; (2) the human thinking about plants; (3) how human thinking is, to some extent, dehumanized and rendered plantlike by its encounter with the vegetal world; and (4) the ongoing symbiotic relation between this transfigured thinking and the existence of plants.[4] A sound philosophy of vegetal life, Marder argues, must rely on a combination of these four. *Estado Vegetal* brings about such philosophy by means of a dramaturgical composition that affords ways of enacting thinking that blur the distinction between philosophy and art. The composition of the piece engages audiences in modes of enacting thinking that destabilize self-evident modes of conceptualizing and invite them to consider how human modes of making sense and thinking, too, happen in interaction with the material world and within a situation of being part of dynamic configurations that include humans as well as matter, and things and other nonhuman elements.

From Thought-Image to Thought-Apparatus

Thought-images (originally in German *Denkbilder*) are not images or pictures; rather, they are short prose texts that aim to evoke mental images as a result of how they engage the reader. The *image* in *thought-image* thus refers to what these writings performatively evoke. Benjamin describes this as a "dialectics at a standstill" that results from how a constellation of elements crystallizes from the linear unfolding of the narrative.[5] The "thought-image" is the result of how the linear progression of the text comes together in a flash as a reader grasps the constellation of elements described in the text, and this grasping is what brings about the mental image. Freddie Rokem has argued that this performativity of the text—how texts evoke images—provides a point of connection between philosophical thinking and theatrical staging. The writing triggers an *Inszenierung* of which the thought-image is the effect.[6]

For Adorno, Benjamin, and other mid-twentieth-century authors, thought-images held the promise of an alternative way of writing history, one that is speculative of how texts do not so much explain things as they engage readers in grasping possible connections between elements presented to them in writing. Adorno describes thought-images as "scribbled picture-puzzles, parabolic evocations of something that cannot be said in words." They establish "a kind of intellectual short-circuiting, which does not hold back conceptual thinking, but shocks through its enigmatic form and by that get thought moving."[7] This way, they can communicate things differently than describing them in words, and perhaps also communicate things that cannot be communicated in words. Performances, it seems, are capable of doing something similar, not by means of how words and writing conjure an *Inszenierung* but by means of a composition of materials, that is, by means of an *actual mise-en-scène*. As compositions of materials in space and time, performances engage audiences in what, with Deleuze and Guattari, we may consider thinking through composition.

In *What Is Philosophy?*, Deleuze and Guattari distinguish between three practices of thinking: philosophy, science, and art. Unlike the title suggests, their book is not so much about the question "what is philosophy?" as it is about the question "what is thinking?" Deleuze and Guattari present what may be called an enactive approach to thinking. Their reflections are not about what thinking in art, science, and philosophy is about; rather, they look at, and reflect on, doing thinking in each of them. Thinking, they argue, involves grasping connections and relations. In philosophy, this takes the shape of the production of concepts, in science of representations of states of affairs, and in art of the creation of compositions. Making sense of a philosophical text, a work of art, or a scientific argument is not a matter of decoding what it represents but is the result of grasping the logic of the act of thought proposed by it. At this point, Deleuze and Guattari's ideas resonate with those of Alfred North Whitehead and his conception of *prehending*.[8] It seems we may conceive of art, science, and philosophy as different ways of prehending, of mediating in different ways of prehending.

Starting with this, we can begin to understand artistic creations as compositions that engage audiences in processes of thinking. Works of art, for example, theatre performances, are compositions in time and space that consist of a diversity of elements (including objects, performers, texts, sounds, light, and more). These compositions engage audiences in grasping, or preheding, the ideas embodied in them. As is the case with thought-images, such thinking is not something *re*presented by the creation but is *brought about* by the material discursive formations set up by the makers. New materialist philosopher Karen Barad observes that human ways of making sense and thinking always happen in interaction with the material world and within a situation of being part of what she describes as *apparatuses*: dynamic configurations that include humans as well as matter, and things and other nonhuman elements. She points to the importance of insights in performativity as developed in social sciences and humanities to further flesh out an understanding of thinking as something that we do in the world, as part of the world and from within a condition of entanglement with the world. Barad does not look at the knowledge and expertise embodied in the arts and in artistic performance. Yet, it seems that much is to be gained from a closer look at contemporary practices of staging and mise-en-scène as examples of thinking understood as a distributed practice in which humans participate as part of larger material discursive configurations. *Estado Vegetal* presents an interesting case because of how the performance engages the audience in speculations about thinking and about relationships of difference between how humans think and what plant-thinking might constitute. The performance does not claim to demonstrate how

plants think; rather, it stages a situation that exposes spectators to the logic of vegetal life and mediates in what philosopher
Michael Marder describes as a "melting into" this logic without
ever becoming identical.[9]

Two Worlds

Marder describes plant-thinking as "the promise and the name of
an encounter" and "an invitation to abandon the familiar terrain
of the human and humanist thought and to meet vegetal life, if not
in the place where it is, then at least halfway."[10] His description
resonates with Barad's book title *Meeting the Universe Halfway:
Quantum Physics and the Entanglement of Meaning and Matter.*
Like Barad, Marder points to the situatedness of thinking: how it
is from the specificities of their bodies and how these bodies operate as part of larger apparatuses that humans and other biological and technical entities make sense of their world. "Whenever
human beings encounter plants, two or more worlds (and temporalities) intersect," observes Marder.[11] The vegetal world is the
world of and for plants. It is the world as accessible to them. As
such, it is fundamentally different from, and inaccessible to, humans and their world. Accepting this difference is important to
respecting the otherness and uniqueness of plants.

Estado Vegetal uses the means of the theatre to expose spectators to these differences via a staged encounter between human
and vegetal worlds. Their staged encounter invites wonder about
how the world might appear to plants: How do plants relate to
the world they encounter? Toward what do they direct themselves? What might they strive for or intend? The performance
begins with a trial situation about an accident that involved a
tree that grew into a power line, causing a short circuit as a result
of which the street lights no longer functioned. In the darkness
that followed, a man on a motorcycle crashed into the tree. The
trial seems to be about determining the exact course of events
and who is to be held responsible. Is the tree to blame for having
been in the way of the motorcycle? Is it the tree that caused the
short-circuiting of the electricity when its branches grew into
the power line, as a result of which the streetlights went dark and
the motorcyclist could not see the tree? Yet, as the one testifying

observes, the tree was there already a long time before the motorcycle, a long time even before the streetlights were installed, and
certainly much earlier than everybody now living in the neighborhood. They came "after the tree. You need to get that order to
understand it." From the perspective of the tree, humans, including the humans who installed the power line and the human on a
motorcycle, failed to acknowledge its already being present there
and how the way they constructed the power line would interfere
with its growth. Blaming the tree for not moving out of the way of
the motorcycle, or for growing into the power line that humans
constructed on a collision course with it, is a denial of the tree's
modes of existence. This denial stands for a much more pervasive
denial of the perspective of plants and their evolutionary first-
ness, as well as for the imposition of a human perspective on the
nonhuman world.

This first scene thus maps out several fundamental differences between the perspective of humans and that of the tree and
draws attention to how this perspective is integrated into human
perceptions of cause and effect and of responsibility. The staged
encounter between these two worlds invites one to consider the
perspective of plants and to imagine what the situation may look
like from their perspective. This is the first way in which the performance mediates in a playful "melting into" the logic of vegetal
life. It invites the human audience to temporarily take up the position of plants, step into their roots, and imagine what the world
looks like from there.

In scenes that follow, the differences between human and vegetal logic are further explored, as is how they relate to different
types of embodiment that afford and inform different modes of
existence, behavior, and ways of thinking. Although all scenes can
be connected in one way or another to the accident and the attempt to work out what happened, they do not add up to one coherent story, nor can the events addressed be merged into one linear
timeline. Instead, time and again, a character or a point of view
introduced in one scene becomes the starting point for a new one,
thus following the plant-based logic of branching out in different
directions. Transitions from one scene to the next do not follow
the logic of hard cuts but that of a gradual morphing of one scene
into the next. This also alludes to a plantlike growth logic. Light

and sound play an important role in making these transitions and in creating a sense of the world of the performance being an ecology in continuous gradual transformation. From the succession of scenes, various lines of association and connections emerge that cut across the scenes and contribute to a sense of increasing density, like a biotope developing over time an increasingly complex web of connections and interrelations, rather than developing in a particular direction. This is the second way in which the construction of the performance invites a "melting into" plant logic. It takes the audience through a story that unfolds according to the logic of plant life and plant behavior and thus mediates a making-experiential of what this logic does and how it differs from human modes of being. This is not a matter of how narrative invites spectators to imaginarily take up the position of plants but of how the composition of the performance invites them to consider a plant-like logic of thinking.

The differences between vegetal logic and human logic are also addressed by the recurrence of the same phrases in different situations. For example, the phrase "Where are your legs?" takes one meaning when used in the context of wonder about plant existence and a quite different one when used in the context of the accident with the motorcycle. The same goes for the expression that is also used as the title of the performance: *Estado Vegetal.* In the performance, this expression describes the existential condition of plants as well as the medical condition of the motorcyclist after the accident. It denotes both the mysterious and by some of the characters desired other of the animal condition and a condition that is inaccessible to humans and frightening. Sometimes these different manifestations collapse, without the differences between them being resolved, for example, when a fireman expresses the wish to become vegetal and then ends up in a vegetative state as a result of an accident. He becomes plant in a metaphorical sense, but this does not mean he has come any closer to being a real plant or in any closer connection to the plant world. It merely means that the human–animal world has lost contact with him.

The performance also suggests a third way of understanding the expression *estado vegetal*—one that is related to the idea of plants taking over the planet—namely, as denoting a mode of governing that is plant based and based on plant logic. We might read the trial scenes at the beginning and ending of the show as referring to such a situation. When the mother of the motorcyclist has a hard time accepting the verdict that no one is guilty and exclaims that it will take her a thousand years to sign the resolution acknowledging this verdict, the plants respond that this is no problem. They have got time—a different sense of time.

"The gap separating humans from plants may dwindle—though not altogether disappear—thanks to the discovery of traces of the latter in the former, and vice versa," Marder observes.[12] This is the third way in which *Estado Vegetal* mediates in a "melting into" the logic of vegetal life. The performance draws attention to how human thinking is haunted by plants and plant life. The text is packed with expressions involving plants, such as "beating around the bush," "sleeping like a log," "being rooted somewhere," and "the leaf of a book." *Estado Vegetal* thus shows plants to be fundamentally part of what philosophers Lakoff and Johnson describe as the metaphors we live by.[13] The expression "argument is war," they argue, is not merely a linguistic expression; it is a metaphor suggesting that argument is partially structured by the concept of war, which is in turn structured by other concepts. These concepts are not just matters of the intellect. They govern our functioning down to the most mundane details of human lives, and they are inseparable from most concrete embodied experience.

The incorporation of plants in ways of speaking and thinking, however, does not mean that we recognize and acknowledge their perspective. On the contrary, claiming that one has been sleeping like a log, for example, may very well imply a human understanding of being a log, and the imposition of this understanding on the log, and thus involve what might be considered a human colonization of "log-experience." Acknowledging the perspective of plants requires recognizing the possibility of plants having a fundamentally different perspective and fundamentally different ways of experiencing that may very well be inaccessible to humans. We cannot know what it means to be a log and how a log experiences this condition, but what we can do is acknowledge the limitations of our human perspective and that when it comes to nonhuman experience, we can only speculate, using human ways of imagining to explore what relationships and differences might be.

Thought-Images and Images of Thinking

Similar to the thought-images of historical writers, the construction of *Estado Vegetal* is unlike a linear unfolding of a narrative; rather, the branching out of the narration in different directions, and the recurrence of the same phrases of text in different situations, contributes to a sense of the linearity of time dissolving into space as the progression of the performance seems to contribute to the crystallization of a composition that grows increasingly complex over time. Ideas, words, images, sounds, objects, and characters become nodes in this composition that does not tell a story but offers the audience a place to imaginarily wander around, listen, and contemplate how they are brought together and what associations and interpretations they trigger. The dramaturgy of the performance thus evokes a sense of geological sedimentation that becomes readable from the other side of time. An example of this is a scene in which the performer, Marcela Salinas, uses a "looping pedal" to create textual circularities. Salinas first records several lines of texts with extended pauses between them. When this text is replayed, she adds lines in between while recording the same sequence again. When this recording is replayed, she adds more lines, and so on. The result is that the linearity of time (the time it takes to record, replay, record, etc.) dissolves into an ever-denser structure that only gradually becomes more understandable.

This coming together to form a constellation is key to the performativity of the texts called thought-images and also to the thinking that underlies their construction. It is through this double perspective of movement and rest, Rokem observes, "that we can achieve what Benjamin terms a 'dialectics at a standstill,' the dynamic stasis through which the *Denkbild* as an image of thought is shaped by the journey of the storyteller that becomes transformed into the movement of the narrative itself."[14] Rokem's observation shifts attention from an understanding of the *Denkbild* as a thought-image toward the *Denkbild* as an image of thought. This shift (which remains unreflected upon in Rokem's text) redirects attention from what the texts called *Denkbilder* performatively bring about (thought-images) toward an understanding of these texts as presenting an image of what it means to think. More precisely, *Denkbilder* present an image of thinking as brought about by interactions between readers and the linearity of written texts and of how these interactions manifest in speculative graspings of connections, as a result of which the linearity of the texts folds back into dynamic constellations of elements or images.

Understood as thought-apparatus, *Estado Vegetal* presents a different image of thinking, namely, of thinking as proceeding in interaction with the theatrical apparatus as a multimodal composition in time and space. Infante explicitly describes her creative practice in terms of thinking with the means of theatre. She observes, "I don't think I would do theatre if it wasn't because I am fascinated with ideas and thinking. I am not fully satisfied by working ideas through just in writing and thinking. That's I think the reason why I do theatre. Not because I want to tell stories or I love the theatre but because it is the way of thinking that works better for me because it is a more embodied and shared form of thinking."[15] Infante describes such thinking as dancing around with ideas, the performances resulting as mappings of this dance after it has happened. "It is a form or architecture, if we would want to use a spatial metaphor. An organization of a path: think of each room as a scene. The only difference is that this is not a path through space but a path through thought, or through sensible experiences, it is by all means a path in time."[16] This path through time that is the composition of the performance embodies the thinking produced in creating it, while, in its turn, it takes the audience along in thinking.

Notes

1. Donna Haraway, "Situated Knowledges: The Science Question in Feminism and the Privilege of Partial Perspective," *Feminist Studies* 14, no. 3 (1988): 575–99.

2. I engage in a more extensive exploration of the idea of theatre as a thought-apparatus in my essay "The Mise en Scene of Posthuman Thinking," *Parse* 12 (Fall 2020), https://parsejournal.com/article/the-mise-en-scene-of-post-human-thinking/, and in "Estado Vegetal—Manuela Infante," in *Doing Dramaturgy: Thinking through Practice,* 181–92 (London: Palgrave Macmillan, 2023).

3. Gerhard Richter, *Thought-Images: Frankfurt School Writers' Reflections from Damaged Life* (Stanford, Calif.: Stanford University Press, 2007), 2.

4. Michael Marder, *Plant Thinking: A Philosophy of Vegetal Life* (New York: Columbia University Press, 2007), 10.

5. Walter Benjamin, *The Arcades Project,* trans. Howard Eiland and Kevin McLaughlin (Cambridge, Mass.: Harvard University Press, 1999), 462.

6. Freddy Rokem, *Philosophers and Thespians: Thinking Performance* (Stanford, Calif.: Stanford University Press, 2010), 172.

7. Theodor W. Adorno, "Benjamin's One Way-Street," in *Notes to Literature* (New York: Columbia University Press, 1991), 2:322.

8. Alfred North Whitehead, *Process and Reality: An Essay in Cosmology* (New York: Free Press, 1978).

9. Marder, *Plant Thinking,* 10.

10. Marder, 10.

11. Marder, 8.

12. Marder, 9.

13. Georg Lakoff and Mark Johnson, *Metaphors We Live By* (Chicago: University of Chicago Press, 1980).

14. Rokem, *Philosophers and Thespians,* 182.

15. Manuela Infante, "The Theatre Has Never Been Human," lecture at the Kyoto Experiment Festival, 2018.

16. Infante.

Manuela Infante and Marcela Salinas, *Estado Vegetal,* 2019. Photograph by Isabel Ortiz. Copyright Manuela Infante.

Theatre as Thinking, Art as Nonknowledge
Lucy Cotter

A few days ago, I found myself in the company of a senior tree consultant, staring up through the branches of the 120-year-old Douglas fir standing by the porch of our recently purchased home in Portland, Oregon. He confided that although trees are expected to follow the same logic in how they grow and behave, they are in fact unpredictable. It had often happened during his forty-year career that a tree whose roots should not have been longer than twenty feet had thirty-foot roots and that these roots had taken detours and made decisions that could not be logically explained. Recounting further stories of dogged individuality, the consultant also warned me that trees do not like change. Even branch pruning alters weight distribution in ways a tree might not appreciate, with potentially dangerous results. Indeed, we had hired this consultant with similar fears about our own tree at the outset of some planned sewer repairs. He confirmed that the related trench digging would likely destabilize our eighty-foot fir, which, if it fell in the wrong direction, could demolish our home. This conversation not only heralded a new plan to reroute the pipe to the road—doubling the project's cost and necessitating a Kafkaesque series of permits with likely delays of many months; it also brought with it a changed perception of our lives. The illusion of owning a sturdy old house buttressed by an age-old guardian tree was replaced by an image of a twenty-four-foot-wide net of roots entangling our piping system and encroaching on our home's structural foundations. Whether we protect it or cut it down, the future impact of that tree on our lives is both inevitable and unknowable.

And so, it was triggering to watch the video documentation of *Estado Vegetal* today, more than two years after I first saw the play in person at the Portland Institute for Contemporary Art. The play's insistence that our separation from plants and their well-being is an illusion we need to be rid of implicated me on a more personal level. The opening scene's observation that trees move all the time, but so slowly that we do not anticipate the force of this operation held new meaning. *Estado Vegetal* renders the reality of planthood tangible to audiences that, like me, have predominantly been socialized through humanistic thinking. It shows us that plants are not under our control; that they are other; that they think and act differently than humans, and we ignore or anthropomorphize them to our own detriment. The half dozen or so protagonists in *Estado Vegetal*—all played by the chameleonic Marcela Salinas—act out the external resonance of this shifting inner reality as their lives intertwine in ways that are circular, synchronistic, and plantlike. A firefighter who spends his days putting out forest fires crashes into a tree on his motorcycle ride home, leading to the vegetative state evoked by the play's title. A woman who talks to trees seems to be a younger version of the old woman who talks to her plants, as time and the sequencing of events become as encircling as a creeper vine.

In her recent work, Infante has processed philosophy's non-human turn and object-oriented explorations, although she characterizes this engagement with "vital materialism" as an extension of her long-term commitment to feminist thought. In its exploration of plant intelligence and the plant as other, Manuela Infante's play *Estado Vegetal* engages more specifically with plant philosophy and plant neurobiology, fields established over the past ten to fifteen years. Plant neurobiologists affirm that plants are cognitive organisms and thus intelligent beings. They "communicate" with neighboring organisms by releasing up to three hundred different chemicals to warn of danger, pests, or drought, among other insecurities.[1] Infante incorporates the findings of Stefano Mancuso—one of the field's pioneers—as well as exploring the ideas of plant philosopher Michael Marder, who notes that "to recognize a valid 'other' in plants is also beginning to recognize that vegetal other within us."[2] Rather than being a metaphor, this is an acknowledgment that human beings are partly made up of plant genomes. There is no division between internal and external when it comes to plant life.

Though all of this makes fascinating material for theatre-making, we should not imagine that *Estado Vegetal* represents or reproduces academic knowledge emerging only from plant philosophy and plant neurobiology, however radical and engaging such an endeavor could be. Rather, to do full justice to what Manuela Infante is undertaking, we need to realize that she shares these disciplines' interest in *other ways of knowing*—that she is thinking with them. As Marder points out, this has not been thought before. Plants have occupied "the zone of absolute obscurity undetectable on the radar of our conceptualities" until very recently.[3] Not only is this shared enthusiasm for unprecedented thought not readily available among plant studies scholars at mainstream universities,[4] but, crucially, through her practice as a maker, Infante is lending existing ideas on plant intelligence a new set of registers of knowledge that are connected to the material, embodied, and conceptual forms inherent to theatre itself. Infante embraces all the formal, sensory, comedic modes available through theatre to manifest plant-thinking as "a non-cognitive, non-ideational, and non-imagistic mode of thinking proper to plants," as Marder describes in *Plant-Thinking: A Philosophy of Vegetal Life.*[5]

Theatre as Knowledge: Placing the Unknown at the Center

The order in which things are imagined is important. I now see a house standing next to a tree, where I previously saw a tree standing next to a house. This changes how I move toward the future. It brings a different set of questions. It forces me to think; indeed, it makes new thought possible. By taking me out of my comfort zone, I am put into conditions that lend me a heightened awareness of my sense of reality as an image that can be shifted in profound ways by momentary experiences. *Estado Vegetal,* too, massages and works toward upending our grasp on reality. In fact, Infante was attracted to theatre because she felt it was a place in which philosophical questions and potentially new ways of thinking, could be tested. She describes theatre as a model world, an experimental world in which real-life forces can be used:

> You can create a little model of a world that uses the same actual forces: time, space, human beings, things. It's the real thing, it's not even a replica of it. You can actually try out philosophical ideas and see what happens. I don't think

what's happening is a representation, I think it's an experimental world.[6]

Theatre offered Infante epistemological and creative intellectual
possibilities for engaging with philosophical and political questions that could not easily be found in academic forms of knowledge production. This included the possibility to incorporate ab-
straction and what she first thought of as a sense of "mystery."[7]
This intuitive grasp later developed into a keen sense of one of the
underlying structural differences between academic and artistic
thought, namely, that art puts the unknown at the center of op-
erations, whereas academic research is premised on the notion
that scholars build on existing knowledge. Academic exceptions
include new disciplines, such as plant neurobiology, which must
arguably think anew, and so it is particularly fertile territory to
think *with* these disciplines as an artist.

Infante is not alone in perceiving theatre in epistemological
terms. Her undertakings can be positioned in relation to the field
of "artistic research," which shifts conceptions of the arts away
from the purview of entertainment and aesthetic exploration for
its own sake toward an understanding that the arts are a form of
knowledge production. The discursive reconfiguration of theatre
in these terms is a relatively recent phenomenon. It takes place
in parallel with comparable shifts in the visual arts that have become established over the past fifteen years, often in tandem with
the development of the doctorate in fine arts degree.[8] Whether in
theatre, visual art, dance, architecture, or music, there is growing recognition of the arts as exceptionally open-ended fields of
creative intellectual inquiry, with various (material, embodied)
registers of knowledge that open possibilities not available in traditional, corporatized university settings. And yet, owing to the
embedded hierarchies in knowledge production, the acknowledgment of artistic research *as research* also brings potential mis-
understandings. There lurks an assumption that the arts act as a
supplement to academic research, illustrating it or creating a more
accessible or entertaining form of conveying academic knowledge
to the wider public. As I have argued elsewhere, this undermines
the potential of the arts to offer not so much a supplement as a
competing framework for how to think and how to research.[9]

When artistic research is viewed through the lens of academic research, the different registers of knowledge artists draw on and manifest in their work get lost in the process. Form is often separated from content, with content becoming the essential and overaddressed factor and form becoming a mere accessory, while the sensory experience of the arts is sidelined or even overlooked.[10] Working in artistic fields that have predominantly distanced themselves from formalism-for-its-own-sake since the 1960s, it has been difficult for contemporary practitioners to articulate how form and research are entangled. This is indeed the most difficult aspect of creative practice to explain to those outside of one's field who have not experienced how ideas might lie in gestures and movement, in sound and space, or in digital and hands-on forms of materiality. The public has little insight into how the intuitive nature of the artistic process allows these material-embodied ideas to co-shape and provide direction for the (theatrical) material in process. Rather than producing formal knowledge through this process, I consider artists' work to produce what Georges Bataille, among other philosophers, has referred to as "nonknowledge." This term evokes the active use of registers of knowledge that are "below the radar of our conscious thought" and "bypass our rational minds."[11]

Indeed, it is the form-based methodologies inherent in the arts that enable an opening out of this level of thought, which is always in flux and can be held open as a fluctuating entity through time-based media.[12] For Infante, formal experimentation through theatre goes hand in hand with experiments in thinking:

I'm a very big fan of formal exploration, so exploring the limits of what theatre can do is fascinating in its own right. I do a lot of work that is devoted just to that. In the 70s, the European avant-garde was able to explore formally what painting was, what theatre was, etc., and now we're sort of "not allowed" to do that anymore, because art has become so instrumental to institutions and politics. I think theatre has become very utilitarian in that sense.[13]

Working with this mode of formal experimentation, Infante has sought ways to embody plantness with the body of the theatre piece itself. Drawing on plant neurobiology, she started to isolate certain concepts around plant behavior, such as modularity, ramification, polyphonic communication, photosynthesis, and phototropy. She was thinking about how to make performance and undermine theatrical norms in those terms. If we look more closely at *Estado Vegetal,* we can see how formal experimentation and the opening of new pathways for knowledge go hand in hand.

The Structure of Thought

My oversight of the living reality of the eighty-foot Douglas fir at my doorstep seems not an unusual state of affairs. Marder argues that our taking for granted of plants, their sheer inconspicuousness and our lack of attention to them in landscaped urban settings, matches their marginalization in philosophical discourse.[14] In the absence of a philosophical tradition proper to planthood, there is a necessary search for ways of thinking the multiplicity and multidirectionality of planthood, which has nothing to do with linear narrative or rational humanistic ordering. To think with plants, therefore, one must imagine or forge a way of thinking that is differently structured. How is it possible to develop such thinking? The conventional structures of academic writing do not lend themselves to such a possibility because they are predicated on a singular rational unidirectional logic.[15] They are formulated in such a way that associative, multidirectional thinking, multiple parallel truths or existences and their inherent contradictions, are difficult to manifest. Here the open-ended thinking and formal experimentation within artistic research can lend other possibilities, as we can see in Infante's work.

One of the exceptional achievements of *Estado Vegetal* is its vegetal structuring of narrative, which lends the play a different shape with which to hold thought, making space for plants' alternative structuring of reality. Moreover, the play's repetitive rhythms, which echo the modularity of plant structures, build on each other to produce otherwise unseeable points of tangential connection and subtle differentiation. The almost obtuse repetition of everyday phrases containing plant-related terms in *Estado Vegetal,* such as "rooted," "planted," and "leaf of a book," takes on force when entire phrases are rearticulated by different characters, creating a circular narrative structure. "I can't move," a statement uttered by a firefighter as he lies on the ground following the motorcycle accident, is later whispered by plants contemplating the dangers of their inherent immobility. These subtle variations and loops echo Gertrude Stein's *Landscape Plays,* with Infante's foregrounding of the medium of writing creating a comparable metadrama. Yet, Infante derives this branching structure from the study of plants, noting how they have evolved within a modular system, with each subpart being different but repeating basic systems—such as breathing apparatuses—to make them more sustainable. This reflects the long evolution of plant DNA, which is older than human DNA. Infante's engagement with these thinking structures is not so much an illustration of how plants think as the opening of new pathways for thought that might enable us to think with plants.

Much of *Estado Vegetal* was not conceived or "written" in an academic or literary fashion but rather evolved using different kinds of improvisation as research tools, in close collaboration with the play's sole human actor and coauthor, Marcela Salinas. The development of the play's structure is the result of a formal experimental process and thus a characteristically open-ended but rigorous form of artistic research. Infante describes their process as follows:

> We did the whole thing using improvisation, but there were a lot of different kinds of improvisation. For example, I would practise branching in a narrative with Marcela.... I said to Marcela: "Tell me a story, starting with any character you want, and whenever you quote somebody else in the story, whenever another human subject comes into the story, you need to branch off into that person." We would practise this branching for hours and hours. Many of the characters came from those branching improvisations.... Many things happened through these really simple exercises. If Marcela said things that I liked, I would write them down, and I was seeing how this branching thing worked so that later I could write it.[16]

As we see from Infante's account, the improvisation process forces new thought, opening a space that is indifferent to the coordinates

of given reality, a kind of no-man's land for thought and materiality in which the unforeseen can be made manifest.[17]

Although the process might appear to be "really simple," its success builds on decades of practice-led knowledge, which mani-
fests as artistic intuition. The conditions for such work also need
to be set in place for such an intuitive and open-ended process to
be fruitful. Among other aspects, Infante notes the importance
of finding collaborators with this level of connection to intuitive
knowledge:

> I always work with actors that are able to allow their con-
> sciousness to flow. I need them to be able to produce material,
> and not to be second-guessing themselves. I always look for
> people that I know can follow their gut feeling and speak it,
> and not be afraid. A lot of the work starts with creating an
> environment to be able to make that happen.[18]

Salinas is the coauthor of *Estado Vegetal,* and the symbiotic relationship between actor and director in this one-person play
is evident throughout. Their intuition-led process of exchange
brings unforeseen material to light that cannot be "thought up"
or "thought" prior to the unfolding of this artistic process. This
collaborative improvisational structure has a particular function
here because plant life is "radically inconceivable" using conventional singular modes of being or thinking.[19] Plants contain multiple internal variations like male and female branches and different leaf shapes or sizes that depend on physiological allocations.[20]
Infante and Salinas create an unprecedented space to explore the
multiplicity of these "semiotic selves" within plant life.[21] Their
working methods generate a discursive structure centered on
multiple, branching, and mutually entangled human experiences,
creating difference within repetition and thus a homology with
the structural reality of plant experience as a multiplicity.

Beyond Otherness: Embodied Knowledge

It is notable that the formal and philosophical multiplicity of
Estado Vegetal is at odds with the post-Enlightenment humanism that underpins mainstream academic knowledge produc-

tion. Infante remarks that "'human' is a concept that has always excluded [her], as a woman, as a lesbian, as a South American."[22] The play's posthumanism consciously facilitates a restructuring of discursive space "to find a new centre, which is not the white straight heterosexual thinker."[23] The play's characters, which emerged during the improvisation process, were all people who are often considered "less than human." "There's a weird little girl, there's a guy that doesn't live in the city, there's a woman who's a mother. It wasn't conscious, but I think we chose characters that were all marginal humans in a way."[24] Challenging the fundamentally hostile grounds of dominant knowledge, *Estado Vegetal* leads the audience to the borders of what constitutes "normality," with the intention of inviting reconsideration of the implicit boundaries between "being human" and "being other." It asks us to straddle the zones of indistinction between the known, the unknown, and the unknowable.

Incorporating crosscutting representations of disability, of aging, and of neurodiversity, Salinas's and Infante's human characters more specifically draw us in to engage with zones of potential otherness as an embodied experience. Gestures and facial expressions move through states of delinquency, infantilism, senility, and mourning. Salinas's often twitchy and jerky movements invoke these states of mental unease. Her transitions from one character to another feel like permutations of the self. They bring home the deep imbrication of plant life within the body through borderline human ways of holding and moving the body in space. In turn, the "vegetative state" in the play's title can be taken to refer to planthood as a vegetal state of being, or as a reference to a brain dysfunction in which a person shows no signs of awareness, recalling the motorcycle crash victim central to the narrative. By creating this ambiguity, the title teases out the border between being and nonhuman states, states of total otherness. In doing so, it makes space for unknowability.

The play's title alludes furthermore to the protagonist of *Rey Planta* (2006), an earlier work by Infante and Teatro de Chile in which a prince who, in a vegetative state following a suicide attempt, is made king and forced to rule without speaking or moving. Infante divided the actors into "the body" and "the voice," with the voice present only via a small monitor or TV set. This experimentation paved the way to later engage with multiplicity in *Estado Vegetal*. Infante goes on to explore the voice as a foremost arena of otherness within the human experience. Rather than being a source of human expression, it is embraced as a zone of embodied nonknowledge at the border of the unknowable. Salinas's use of her voice acts as a container for much of this insoluble material. In her breathing and vocal sounds, she alludes to the existence of nonanthropocentric languages. Sometimes she draws on the facial expressivity of mime, which can capture moments just preceding articulation or material that is on the brink of being representable. *Estado Vegetal* is a Spanish-language play, accompanied by projected subtitles in English. Yet this language barrier is not an obstacle to this immersive experience, perhaps because Salinas's words offer only a fraction of the play's expressive interest. Indeed, the intonation and pitch of Salinas's voice approach whistling and birdsong at times, even as she is "speaking."

This multiplicity of voice–body relations echoes the polyphonic nature of plant communication, which involves chemical messages that can be "smelled" by other plants. At several moments, Salinas harmonizes her voice through a layering that gestures toward plant communication. Hence "the chemical polyphony translates in the show as breaking into musical harmony."[25] Infante, who is also a musician, sees theatre per se as a bringing together of music and philosophy because "it happens as an unfolding of rhythm through time and space."[26] By extension, the sound effects she developed for this play are not only theatrical but, in addition, manifest distinct philosophical possibilities. Among them, the use of a looper pedal makes the actor's voice reflect the inherent multiplicity of vegetal structures, rather than affirming individualized existence. This technologically mediated device offers a way of thinking that has a nonlinear relationship to time. During the writing process, Infante asked herself, "What does it mean to write in layers? Piling time onto each other instead of moving forward."[27] Materialized using artistic tools like the looper, the multiple circular narratives in *Estado Vegetal* reject progression. This is an act of philosophical and political refusal, which invites other approaches, not only to narrative in playwriting, but to thinking as such.

The potential of theatre as a form of thinking that encompasses the logic of rhythm and sensory registers of knowledge more broadly speaking is evident across the three plays and the sonic opera that Infante has created since *Estado Vegetal*. *Eloquence* (2019), her sonic opera, delves more deeply into electronic live processing and layering of voices to produce soundscapes.[28] *Metamorphoses* (2021), a "noise play," investigates the voice, not an expression of human agency but a "more-than-human thing" that "entangles humans and non-humans in endless ventriloquisms, refrains and echoes, without ever belonging to either."[29] With *Noise* (2021), Infante has investigated "what is heard in the background and what is heard in the foreground—and what eludes this classification."[30] Each of these works further elaborates a music-philosophical exploration of the borders between living and non-living entities through sound. We see theatre here opening the way for thinking that is not conceptual but an embodied knowledge that bypasses thought as such.

Moving into other sensory realms that exceed the limits of language, Infante extends *Estado Vegetal*'s experimentation with plant intelligence to include several other aspects that exceed human narrative structures. Let me briefly highlight how the play also shifts us away from conventional human motor responses to light and space, leaving behind theatrical conventions of lighting always following the protagonists' actions. Infante collaborated with the play's designer, Rocío Hernández to develop a lighting plan that was closer to plant thinking:

> We talked a lot about phototropy, about how plants are always moving towards the light, whereas in theatre the light follows the actors. We made a rule that the light would move when the actress was still, and the actress would move when the light was still so that they never happened together. We did silent improvisations to try out this idea of light changes. We practised it a lot, and the best moments came out of that practice.[31]

Through their collaboration, Hernández and Infante open a space that cannot be thought as such. By taking up light as a means to explore phototropy, they materialize some of the possibilities for new ways of thinking invoked by posthumanist thinkers like Bruno Latour, who asks in *Reassembling the Social,* "When we act, who else is acting?" and "How many agents are also present?"[32] Throughout her work, Infante applies these questions quite literally to acting, showing theatre's epistemological potential as an experimental space in which real-life forces can be used.

Humor and Nonknowledge

Exceeding our rational conception, we tend to react physically when we pass momentarily into the truly unknown. This leads us to the affective force of theatre, and the arts at large, which often contain nonknowledge—knowledge that has difficulty making a home in the environment of academic thought. In an essay titled "Nonknowledge, Laughter and Tears," Bataille proposes that nonknowledge cannot be examined independently of the effects it produces, which are more likely to be affective or bodily reactions than rational thoughts.[33] He has brilliantly observed the role of laughter as a signal of this movement from a state of knowing to a state of unknowing. Infante, too, understands the agency of such moments. She observes, "Laughing is just the body being moved from one place to another. I use laughter as a very strong tool to know what to keep. I use other tools but when I'm in rehearsal and I'm laughing, I follow that path."[34] It is often through absurd and even slapstick humor that the performance digs into and hacks at humanist self-conceptions and a widely shared underestimation of the importance of plants to planetary well-being.

Toward the beginning of *Estado Vegetal,* Salinas momentarily becomes an old woman who converses and flirts with her houseplants with the intimacy of a "real" relationship. This hilarious episode takes an unexpected turn toward the absurd when the plants start to make demands, beginning with the insistence that their pots be placed on the ground. Her subsequent removal of all the floorboards to enable the plants to root in the earth leads to her home's ultimate disappearance in a jungle of weeds. The laughter provoked in the audience by such tales is not only a response to tragicomedy, however. Though the same narrative told as an individual concern might appear as a personal tragedy, Infante never allows her audience to separate the personal from

the political. Given the marginal status of the human beings involved, as well as the looming threat of planetary collapse inform-
ing the narrative at large, the play's humor relates more closely to
a mode that Gilles Deleuze and Félix Guattari refer to as "minor."
Exemplified for them by Kafka's work, "minor literature" burrows
out paths within dominant modes of writing to deny the apparent
space between individual and political expression.[35] Infante uses
it to create modes of thinking that seek to incorporate excluded
positions for knowledge production.

Estado Vegetal's comic effect is not always immediate; rather,
it lingers when the significance of passing, often absurd words is
digested. When the old lady asks her plant, "If we were to sing the
national anthem now, where would you put your hand?," language
leaves behind its representative function and moves instead toward its extremities and its limits.[36] As it moves, it effects a deterritorialization of thought and, by extension, it deterritorial-
izes the conditions for (political) representation. The embedded
humor shares minor literature's claustrophobic relationship to
politics, its critical political stance and "revolutionary" potential.[37] The specter of revolution is heralded directly on occasion
via seemingly silly questions, such as "If we were to decapitate
you, where would we cut?" This imagery of decapitation is, in the
first instance, political. At the same time, being "headless" offers a metaphoric return to epistemological possibilities. Marder
devotes several pages to analyzing how the headless existence of
plants invokes a Bataillean invocation of the headless discourse
production of dense non-sense.[38]

The parodic undoing of sense is at other times wordless. In a
later monologue, Salinas comments on human mortality, observ-
ing how "everything that lives eventually has to die" and asking
"if you never die, how can you say you are alive?" Yet, though the
words appear serious and normative, she speaks them while absurdly dressed as a fake plastic plant. This parodic humor eats
into and destabilizes the inherent humanistic thinking, consti-
tuting space for nonknowledge to enter the equation. We are led
to laugh at ourselves, and through this means, we are prepared
for the reality that plants "silently deconstruct metaphysics," as
Marder observes in Plant-Thinking.[39] Rather than viewing the
internal shifting brought about by laughter that is simultaneous

with nonknowledge as a self-contained happening, this unfolding is a continuous operation of loosening parameters that have become fixed. It utilizes the malleability of thought as a form and, by extension, the formability of institutions. It renders tangible the fluidity of private beliefs that manifest in public and political structures.[40] Indeed, the distributed organization of tasks in planthood offers an alternative model of organization and governance, which is constantly inferred.

Nonknowledge, after Thought

Looking out at the 120-year-old Douglas fir that pushes my thoughts in unexpected directions, I realize that the unexplainable detours and durations of plant growth are simply a reflection that plants do not follow a logic imposed by human systems of understanding. In this light, the word *knowledge* seems to evoke something too easily discernible relative to *Estado Vegetal*'s nomadic furrowing into plant life's multiple depths. Consciously extending the parameters of *Estado Vegetal* beyond rational thinking, Infante insists that "there's a lot of space for obscurity, for things you can't access or make sense of," aiming to foreground "that which cannot dissolve into human knowledge."[41] What Infante produces through *Estado Vegetal* is thus not so much knowledge in the standard conception of the term as a journey to and beyond the limits of knowledge. As Bataille has observed, if you engage deeply with the domain of knowledge in any field, you come to reach its limit and arrive on the other side of that knowledge into a kind of nonknowledge. What lies on the other side of that limit is not only what is not yet known but also what is unknowable.[42]

We are never far from the purview of academic thought, however. Nor does Infante hide her interest in philosophy per se, which emerges most strongly in the firefighter's monologue on the relationship between language and planthood. However, she invokes her struggle with the citational logic of academic thought structures: "As if the words themselves were leaves, citations of other leaves." Nonknowledge always signals these limits of formal knowledge production, yet one "re-enter[s] categories of knowledge while straddling nonknowledge."[43] If we consider the arts and theatre's broader relationship to knowledge in this manner, we start to understand why artistic research might overlap with research in other fields yet not provide *supplementary* knowledge; rather, artists offer contributions that distinguish themselves both in their aims and in their outcomes, often posing questions about the frameworks of existing discourses. Following Aristotle, Marder argues that "the human who thinks like a plant literally becomes a plant since the destruction of the classical logos annihilates the thing that distinguishes us from other living beings."[44] In turn, the human being in an *estado vegetal,* a vegetable-like state, "is not one who no longer thinks but, in a more nuanced formulation, one who thinks without following the prescriptions of formal logic and therefore, in some sense, thinks without thinking."[45] The intuitive and imaginative aspects of Infante's *Estado Vegetal* are difficult to articulate in words, precisely because they bring us off the radar of thinkable territory. As Deleuze observes more generally, what matters in art is "never what is known but rather a great destruction of what is already known, in favor of the creation of the unknown."[46] It is this creative-destructive act that lends *Estado Vegetal* a haunting force that not only changes our perception of planthood but bears the potential to affect the way we think about or engage with the unknown and unknowable within and beyond any subject.

Notes

Research for this chapter was funded in part by the Regional Arts and Culture Council.

1. See Michael Pollan, "The Intelligent Plant: Scientists Debate a New Way of Understanding Flora," *New Yorker,* December 15, 2013, https://www.newyorker.com/magazine/2013/12/23/the-intelligent-plant.

2. Michael Marder, cited by Manuela Infante during a lecture titled "Post-human Theatre" held at Portland Institute for Contemporary Art, Portland, Oregon, April 27, 2019.

3. Michael Marder, *Plant-Thinking: A Philosophy of Vegetal Life* (New York: Columbia University Press, 2013), 2.

4. This kind of imaginary freedom is difficult to sustain within the university context because academic research is expected to follow the traditional academic protocol of building on existing knowledge. Furthermore, academic fields are especially territorial in the corporatized university system, challenged by how new ways of thinking might reconfigure the status

of existing research and its funding possibilities and how scientific reputations impact academic careers and job security. A brief overview of how plant neurobiology has been received within plant studies can be found in Pollan, "Intelligent Plant."

5. Marder, cited by M. Infante.

6. Lucy Cotter and Manuela Infante, "Performance as Philosophy: A Dialogue with Manuela Infante," in *Reclaiming Artistic Research,* ed. Lucy Cotter (Berlin: Hatje Cantz, 2019), 321.

7. Cotter and Infante.

8. For a survey of this development, see Danny Butt, *Artistic Research in the Future Academy* (Bristol, U.K.: Intellect, 2017).

9. See Cotter, *Reclaiming Artistic Research.*

10. I discuss this separation in, among other texts, "Reclaiming Artistic Research: First Thoughts . . . ," *MaHKUscript Journal of Fine Art Research* 2, no. 1 (2018), Article 1, https://www.mahkuscript.com/articles/10.5334 /mjfar.30/.

11. I draw on Sarat Maharaj's definition of "non-knowledge," from a workshop as part of Cork Caucus, 2005, curated by Art/Not-Art, Charles Esche, and Annie Fletcher.

12. I explore many of these aspects of art in my book in progress, "Art Knowledge: Between the Known and the Unknown."

13. Cotter and Infante, "Performance as Philosophy," 323–24.

14. Marder, *Plant-Thinking,* 4.

15. That more and more academics are turning to artistic forms to further their work suggests this. This includes, but is not limited to, academics engaging with questions around race, sexuality, and gender who seek better formats with which to explore and communicate embodied knowledge.

16. Cotter and Infante, "Performance as Philosophy," 326–27.

17. In my formulation, I draw on Peter Hallward's reference to Gilles Deleuze's reflections on art as a site for thinking. Hallward, *Out of This World: Deleuze and the Philosophy of Creation* (London: Verso, 2006), 106.

18. Laurel V. McLaughlin, "*Estado Vegetal,* a Gesture of Imitation: An Interview with Manuela Infante," *Performance Research* 25, no. 2 (2020).

19. I draw on Eduardo Kohn, *How Forests Think: Toward an Anthropology beyond the Human* (Berkeley: University of California Press, 2013), 86.

20. See Carlos M. Herrera, *Multiplicity in Unity: Plant Subindividual Variation and Interaction with Animals* (Chicago: University of Chicago Press, 2009).

21. I borrow this term from Kohn, who uses it to consider Ecuador's Upper Amazon forests as "an ecology of selves." Kohn, *How Forests Think,* 78.

22. Cotter and Infante, "Performance as Philosophy," 323.

23. Cotter and Infante, 323.

24. Cotter and Infante, 327.

25. Cotter and Infante, 332.

26. This observation from a Spanish-language video interview with Alejandra Costamagna is cited by Fabian Escalona, "Manuela Infante Makes Space for Ideas," *American Theatre,* April 22, 2019, https://www.americantheatre.org/2019/04/22/manuela-infante-makes-space-for-ideas/.

27. Cotter and Infante, "Performance as Philosophy," 331. Indeed, as she notes in the dialog, this became a departure point for her subsequent play *How to Turn to Stone* (2020), which involved thinking in sedimented structures.

28. See "Eloquence: A Sonic Opera by Director Manuela Infante," *The T:>Works Blog,* undated, https://theatreworkssg.wordpress.com/2019/11/04/eloquence-a-sonic-opera-by-director-manuela-infante/.

29. *Metamorphoses,* KVS, Brussels, 2021, https://www.kvs.be/en/agenda/454/Manuela_Infante_Michael_De_Cock_Diego_Noguera_KVS/Metamorphoses.

30. I cite Felicitas Arnold, "When the Background Becomes the Foreground Becomes the Background," 2021, https://www.schauspielhausbochum.de/en/news/8124/when-the-background-becomes-the-foreground-becomes-the-background.

31. Cotter and Infante, "Performance as Philosophy," 327.

32. Bruno Latour, *Reassembling the Social: An Introduction to Actor-Network-Theory* (Oxford: Oxford University Press, 2008).

33. Stuart Kendall, *The Unfinished System of Nonknowledge Literature,* ed. Georges Bataille (Minneapolis: University of Minnesota Press, 2001), 137.

34. Cotter and Infante, "Performance as Philosophy," 337.

35. See Gilles Deleuze and Félix Guattari, *Kafka: Towards a Minor Literature* (Minneapolis: University of Minnesota Press, 1986).

36. I draw here on Deleuze and Guattari's articulation of these qualities in Kafka's writing in *Kafka,* 23.

37. Deleuze and Guattari argue that the minor suggests "the revolutionary conditions for every literature within the heart of what is called great (or established) literature" (18).

38. Marder refers to a particularly Bataillean passage in Jean-Luc Nancy, *Corpus* (2008). Marder, *Plant-Thinking,* 62–64.

39. Marder, 56.

40. Infante explains that "rather than having a central government, plants have governments in every leaf and root. So, plants make collective decisions that happen to be individual." Unpublished material from the author's recorded conversations with Infante, 2019.

41. Q&A following *Estado Vegetal,* with Manuela Infante and Marcela Salinas, moderated by Craig Epplin, Portland Institute for Contemporary Art, April 26, 2019.

42. Cotter, "Art Knowledge."

43. Kendall, *Unfinished System,* 116.

44. Marder, *Plant-Thinking,* 165.

45. Marder.

46. Gilles Deleuze, cited by Hallward, *Out of This World.*

Manuela Infante and Marcela Salinas, *Estado Vegetal,* 2019. Photograph by Isabel Ortiz. Copyright Manuela Infante.

Vegetal Mythologies
Potted Plants and Storymaking
Giovanni Aloi

October. Chicago. At this time of the year, I keep an ear out for the lonely songs of the last cicadas. The rattling choruses that filled the warm summer air at dusk fizzle and wane as the end of September ushers in the first autumn showers. Sunlight gets paler—it burns the skin but no longer warms the air. Shadows grow longer across the garden. The first chilly nights slow down both plant and insect life at once.

The song of the last cicada heralds the first yellow leaves. Much more accurately than any other horticultural calendar, these cues tell me it's time. From here on, the bold glory of summer afternoons fades into distant memory. The scent of ripening promises that filled the summer air turns into a moist mélange of relentless decay. It's time to prune and tidy up. It's time to remove and dismantle. Cover and shelter.

These autumn days in the garden are tough: the opposite of those joyful mid-March mornings when, in Chicago, first some timid crocuses, then the sun-kissed winter aconites bravely break the freshly thawed ground in search of sun. I admire their strength and determination. A palpable urgency to be alive is rooted deep in them. A week later, the ground erupts into shimmering shades of blue as scilla and dwarf irises compete for the attention of early pollinators. Spring brims with an uncontainable vegetal exuberance accumulated under wintery layers of ice and snow. In the warming afternoons, every petal drips desire.

Daffodils and tulips swiftly set the garden ablaze in shades of yellow, orange, and red. Icons of resilience, they weather the occasional late frost—unscathed. Then, often too soon, their heads bow down to the ground. Another cue. Time has come once again to migrate more than a hundred pots from the basement out into the garden—agaves, cacti, poinsettias, hibiscuses, palms, and angel trumpets. Up and down the stairs, with my heart intoxicated by the promise of summer gloat, I don't feel the weight, don't sense the wear.

A couple of days later, once again, the garden is whole. The tropical plants that spent six months under the stern glare of grow lights look ready for their summer lusting. It's hard not to anthropomorphize. Though they do pretty well—some even bloom—in their winter abode, nothing suits them better than true sunlight, rain, dew, and warm breezes.

This is also a time for repotting the plants that have fast out-grown their radical comfort. I gently pull, wiggle, and lift the plants out. At times, like gesso poured into a mold, roots have faithfully cast the innards of the pot. Depending on the species, gardening literature advises to break up this tight, radical en-twinement to promote fresh root growth and facilitate the ab-sorption of oxygen and nutrients.

Repotting makes one painfully aware of the oddness of pots. We often take them for granted, but they are peculiar objects. They have always been around us. They are everywhere a plant should not be. They are a quintessential feature in most homes and gardens, as well as offices and corporate lobbies, and they are the only reason garden centers exist. Pots make plants mobile. They radically alter their sessile nature—the characteristic that in our minds most prominently distinguishes plants from us and other animals. Pots also isolate plants from other plants. Recent research has shown that plants communicate with each other through their root systems and the mycelia that grow on them.[1] How does a pot limit or alter the essential vegetal being of a plant?

Pots also allow us to monetize plants—they are essential to the chain of production and consumption driving a business that in the United States alone is worth more than $100 billion—twice the value of the global art market. Pots can objectify plants. Through them we claim ownership upon them. Some of us move pots here and there according to our interior design tastes and needs. But pots are also objects of care. The kinship we build with our most beloved houseplants comes in the shape of pots.

I attended a performance of Manuela Infante's *Estado Vegetal* in 2019[2] and have since been unable to overlook the intricate cul-

tural and ethical complexities that something as seemingly innocent as a plant pot can raise. While pots appear onstage here
and there throughout the play, a scene in which Nora—an elderly
lady—is ordered by her plants to free them from their pots has
haunted my gardening ever since.

It is known that clay and ceramic pots were widely used in
India, Japan, China, and Korea more than three thousand years
ago, but mostly to bring plants closer to houses and into court-
yards rather than indoors. Terra-cotta plant pots have been found
in the Minoan palace at Knossos on Crete.[3] The Romans preferred
to plant lemon trees in large marble pots. And throughout the
Middle Ages, pots were used in convents to grow herbs and to
keep life-saving medicinal plants close at hand.

Pots became instrumental to the rise of botanical gardens in
Europe and to the growth in popularity of orangeries and, eventually, heated glass greenhouses. As Europe's colonialist ambitions
expanded throughout the eighteenth century, trade in spices, tea,
coffee, chocolate, sugar, and tobacco dramatically increased, as
did the demand for live exotic plants. European aristocrats rel-
ished the opportunity to impress their friends and guests with
glorious greenhouses. Plants can be sought-after status symbols.

The lure of the exotic has always appealed to kingly power. The
oldest botanic gardens and menageries owned by Middle East-
ern and Italian kings were a spectacle affirming the kings' super-
natural power over creation and, by implication, over people.
Louis XIV owned more than a thousand orange trees, each planted
in a large clay pot. The pots were transferred to heated greenhouses in winter.

In autumn especially, as I pick up each pot and make my way
back into the basement, these genealogies crowd my mind as I
ask myself if they still play a role, perhaps subliminally, in what I
do. Is it care or torture to take my plants into a basement for the
winter long haul? Are pots vegetal torture devices par excellence
or vessels of care?

Returning each plant to the basement at the end of summer is
all about the force of gravity—the downward pull is overpowering.
The process lacks all the joy and enthusiasm that, in early spring,
had propelled the plants' return to the open air. I push myself and
my plants to the limit as I unrealistically aim to take them in at

the very last minute, often just a few hours before temperatures drop below the low thirties. I try to let them enjoy the open air as much as possible, but as a result, the homing process often turns out to be rushed and messy. I have done this many times under the pouring rain, making the most of the only useful window of time between unmovable work commitments. Moving the pots is exhausting; they are heavier than in early spring when I took them out. The plants have grown, and cold autumn rain has soaked the soil. It is through this mournful process, as I trace my steps downward a hundred times over, that I wonder about the sense of all this: the effort, the work, the struggle, the heartbreak.

Of course, one could easily argue that my life as a gardener would be much simpler if I gave up all the plants that don't naturally grow in this climate. There would be no plants in the basement to worry about while traveling during the winter holidays, and neither would I be spending time containing the unavoidable mite and aphid infestations that regularly break out in February. But the question is not necessarily one of native versus exotic cultivars. Yes, life would be simpler, but it would also be emptier, much emptier.

Vegetal Mythologies

Some of us are very aware that plants can simultaneously be appreciated for their aesthetic beauty, behavior, and complexity and for the ways in which they carve special places in the kinds of memories that define our identities. *Vegetal mythologies* are a form of personal fiction that gives structure to our lives while supporting a sense of self. Like the mythical tales central to ancient Japanese, Indian, and Chinese cultures, or to classical Greece, these narratives are filled with nonhuman and human characters woven into reality and yet charged with a sense of magical enchantment that surpasses the predictability of nature's laws. Vegetal mythologies magnify the memory of certain plant encounters carving a special place in our shared autobiographies.

In the opening of my coauthored book *Why Look at Plants? The Botanical Emergence in Contemporary Art,*[4] I recalled how the potted plants my grandmother grew in the south of Italy have impacted my relationship with the vegetal world:

pansies, variegated petunias, the sculptural dish-like foliage of leopard plants, red geraniums, deep red gloxinias, tall ferns, fuzzy fern-asparagus, a giant rubber plant, slender orange and yellow zinnias, African daisies, sharp mother-in-law tongues, dark-leaved Irish roses, two small palms, nasturtium, nasturtium, nasturtium, and a bonsai-like money-tree.[5]

These are only some of the plants that today have become staples in my home and garden. Hibiscuses and angel trumpets also occupy a prominent place in a series of vegetal mythologies that bridge faraway places, plants, time, and people—my roots are intertwined with those of the plants that populated my childhood or with others that for one reason or another have become part of my own mythologies along the way. Vegetal mythologies can develop at any time in one's life. They are markers of meaningful moments, moments of shared growth.

But most importantly, vegetal mythologies pry open epistemological spaces between scientific thinking and Western philosophy. This interstice is ripened with an epistemological potential we have been taught to disregard as romantic or irrelevant. It is here, in this space, that we can reclaim ourselves and our first-hand experiences as legitimate and valid sources of important knowledge.

Vegetal mythologies don't necessarily anthropomorphize the plant, but they personalize the relationship to the point that plants become irreplaceable individuals. Plants can be propagated via seeds and cuttings. Among others, these methods allow the same plant to become ubiquitous—a living lineage that connects people across faraway places.

Multiple and yet individual—I still have an *Echeveria lilacina* that descends from a plant owned by my grandmother, who passed away in the late 1990s. In the 1970s, she gave my mum a rooted cutting to take with her to Milan. And my mum gave me a couple of cuttings to take to London with me in the 1990s. I then took a few rooted leaves with me to Chicago in 2014. This echeveria has become an emblem of the stories of immigration that have shaped my family. The plant is still thriving. It's not exactly the same plant my grandmother passed on to my mother. No leaf or branch from that time still exists. And yet it is. It is the sum of their love for each other and of mine for them crystallized into living vegetal form. Despite looking similar, a replacement plant of the same species could never occupy the same biographical space. Neither could I just gift a cutting of it to someone who did not care for, nor understand, the affective bond this plant embodies in my vegetal mythology. Some plants can become living relics—connections to loved ones that are no longer within reach. These plants are among the most precious, and yet they can be as cheap as chips at the gardening center.

British painter Lucian Freud received a cutting of zimmerlinde *(Sparrmannia africana)* from his father, the son of the father of psychoanalysis, Sigmund Freud. Not only did Lucian paint the plant over and over in his work but many of his children still have a potted zimmerlinde that grew from the original cutting Sigmund passed on to Lucian's father Ernst before he moved to London from Austria as he fled the Nazis in the early 1930s. The plant has become a personal family emblem and guardian of a vegetal bloodline intimately linking generations. I saw Lucian Freud's zimmerlinde in 2018 while doing research for my book *Lucian Freud Herbarium.*[6] Freud passed away in 2011, and I never had the opportunity to meet him. David Dawson, the artist's assistant, still takes care of the plant. It might sound silly, because I know that the artist's touch is embedded in the layers of paint encrusting every one of his enormously expensive canvases, but it was through that encounter with his zimmerlinde that I felt the closest I could possibly have to the artist.

Twice a year, first up the stairs, then down again to the basement, it is not just potted plants that I move back and forth but my life with them—my past, the cities I lived in, and, with them, many human and nonhuman kin that have made it what it is. The potted plants can never just be trivialized as tokens or souvenirs. In their vegetal livingness lies an impossible continuation of a past that cannot die—a nonlinear condensation of time, words, places, and gestures that can only truly manifest when the honeysuckle will bloom again. Nothing like its overly sweet scent summons the memory of summer evenings spent listening to my grandmother's stories—her honeysuckle in a large pot framing the door to the kitchen.[7] The memory it summons is not just that of my grandmother but of a becoming in which smell, storytelling, and affect indissolubly entwined in my own growth—the core of single formative experiences in which each part is indispensable to the whole.

Storymaking and Minor Literatures

The plant–human relationships inscribed in vegetal mythologies are never descriptive or literal—they can never be replaced by photographs or inanimate objects. They reach beyond the power of indexicality and its fetishizations, promising encounters with colors, forms, and scents that will appear in a future only the plant owns. As Potawatomi plant ecologist Robin Wall Kimmerer puts it, "we need to un-earth the old stories that live in a place and begin to create new ones, for we are storymakers, not just story-tellers."[8] Personal mythologies can begin with ancestral stories, but they don't have to. They don't need to begin with a tribe or the idea of a better past either. The only thing expected of them is their connection through a deeply personal, and yet sharable, form of storymaking.

As a form of storymaking based on a human–nonhuman co-authoring process, vegetal mythologies bear some similarities to Gilles Deleuze and Félix Guattari's theorization of a *minor litera-ture*: a style of writing that politically resists the cultural main-stream, the writing styles and genres complying with the nor-mativity that defines the literary canon. But most importantly, "the primary characteristic of a minor literature involves all the ways in which the language is effected by a strong co-efficient of deterritorialization."[9] First and foremost, vegetal mythologies re-sist the narrativizing and objectifying rhetoric of gardening lit-erature according to which a plant predominantly is an aesthetic matter or, in the case of vegetables, a provision. They also deter-ritorialize language by pushing it to the extreme of a poetic regis-ter that can never be fully or even adequately transposed into the linguistic register alone. And they also do not belong to the other institutionalized clusters of conversations on mental health and physical well-being that surround the defined commercialization of capitalist antidotes. In that sense, vegetal mythologies belong to a radically minor kind of often unwritten human–nonhuman storymaking that cannot be pegged to a genre, mostly because, as Deleuze and Guattari argue, minor literatures are by nature connective—they are plugged into a subversive plurality with collective value that is always and ultimately political. At the core of vegetal mythologies lies a drive for emancipation of the voice of the individual, not as an anthropocentric monologue, but as a polyvocal arrangement: a nonhuman–human becoming.[10]

Minor literatures resist interpretation, most especially the kind of interpretation that has structured Western epistemology since the rise of humanism—the predictable and relentless mobilization of cultural archetypes and the decoding of symbolism. They challenge the dominant role of the central interpreter as holder of an ultimate truth. To Deleuze and Guattari, interpretation "massacres desire."[11] The acknowledgment of an alternative knowledge that at least in part remains uninterpretable often enables the mapping of rhizomatic continuities that implicitly respects the otherness of the nonhuman, incorporating it but not smothering it into discourses that allow its dignity to remain intact.

Much of the objectification imposed on plants by scientific knowledge through the absolute clarity of positivistic realism in botanical illustration relied on a process of transcription—a forcing of the plant into language. In *Discipline and Punish,* Michel Foucault explores the intrinsic panoptic power of the royal menageries from which the early knowledge of natural history was produced:

> But one finds in the programme of the Panopticon a similar concern with observation, with characterization and classification, with the analytical arrangement of space. The Panopticon is a royal menagerie; the animal is replaced by man, individual distribution by specific grouping and the king by the machinery of a furtive power. With this exception, the Panopticon also does the work of a naturalist.[12]

To Foucault, the epistemic relationship between what is *seen* by the discipline of natural history and what can be *said* is central to the unavoidable shortcomings of representation. In the opening of

The Order of Things, he states that "it is in vain that we say what we see; what we see never resides in what we say."[13] This very gap between seeing and saying opens a space in which disciplines produce knowledge, and it is this very epistemological space that we, as individuals, must reclaim to redefine the discourse.[14]

Natural history, Foucault argues, emerged as an intrinsically reductive system that views nonhuman beings through a grid of knowledge.[15] The emergence of new spatializations of visuality proposed by *spaces of juxtaposition* like herbaria, collections, and gardens during the seventeenth century has in time defined what we could say about the kind of visibility we impose on the natural world.[16]

The rise of the major literature of natural history was defined by a process of *limiting and filtering* of the visible that enabled the transcription of objects into linguistic systems, thus compressing the nonhuman into disciplinary discourse.[17] As a precursor of zoology, the study of botany at once captured the inside and outside of beings, for plants were then understood to "wear their organs on the outside."[18] This condition encapsulates the reductive epistemological modality of the seventeenth and eighteenth centuries by which it was only possible to know and to say what could be ordered within a taxonomic area of visibility.[19]

The herbarium, as a site of knowledge of the vegetal world, outlined a spatialization in which, representationally, all that is epistemologically essential about a plant could be exhaustively transposed into language. Only what could be transposed into language would then become part of disciplinary knowledge—a translation from the optical to the linguistic. The rest was confined to the darkness of irrelevance of nonknowledge, folklore, and other marginalia. It was on the page of early botanical and natural history treatises that the same line that drew the specimen also transcribed into words its essential qualities. The centrality of language as well as the limitations that its structural condition imposes have defined not only the kind of knowledge that can be produced about the natural world but also its scope. It seems therefore particularly pertinent that minor literatures, like vegetal mythologies, involving plant–human relations should intentionally attempt to decentralize the primacy of language to map alternative territories while retaining their elusiveness and idiosyncrasies.

Like Franz Kafka's texts, which Deleuze and Guattari use to exemplify the essence of minor literatures, Manuela Infante's polyvocal monologue that underpins *Estado Vegetal* emerges from a deterritorialization of language induced by traumatic events triggered by uncontrollable changes. In *Estado Vegetal*, the soliloquial linearity of language is fragmented and multiplied into a collective assemblage of enunciations that reverberates into the voices of different individuals, crowds, humans, and nonhumans. This theatrical minor literature devised by Infante foregrounds plants with agency. It allows them to define the form, content, structure, and rhythm of the performance. It is this very eradication of theatrical and literary conventions that enables Infante to deliver a poignantly political and yet poetic proposal.

As narratives intertwine like root entanglements, *Estado Vegetal* casts deep shadows simultaneously on the performative sharpness and adequacy of langue and on our hubristic sense of self that derives from language. From beginning to end, the polyvocal monologue, acted with impetus and wit by actress Marcela Salinas, diffracts identity, connects, and maps new territory at the fringes of philosophical and scientific discourses.

Estado Vegetal leads the viewer through a journey of existential questioning in which the normative boundaries of our cultural anthropocentric sphere are made to crumble scene after scene. This line of inquiry connotes the collective assemblage of enunciation operating in *Estado Vegetal* as a kind of productive *madness,* an induced state of vulnerability that can lead us past our anthropocentric conceptions of rationality and order.

Madness and the Potted Plant

As I walk up and down the stairs carrying pots of varying sizes under the pouring rain, I can't help but wonder about my own sanity and the normative structures that define normality in our relationship with plants. Seven years ago, when I began to plan the garden in our new home, my neighbor would peek over the fence for occasional and often pleasant chattering. However, one day, she said, "Gardening is not how I like to spend my time"—a brisk reminder that we gardeners and plant lovers are a minority and that many people would consider my efforts to keep plants happy foolish at best. In their eyes, our foolishness is manyfold. The time, the effort, the expense, the emotional investment—many people find the last more unsettling than the rest. After all, we have been educated to ignore plants—to feel no obligation or responsibility toward them. Plant blindness is very real,[20] and in the normative scale of formative values that defines the West, one's time, money, and effort are meant to be geared toward greater and profitable things: things like cars, phones, social media, luxury objects, and keeping up with the Kardashians—perhaps coincidently, only one of these might at times involve doing work under the pouring rain, and none have to do with plants. Hobbies—the pastimes invented by capitalism to distract us from the dysfunctionality induced by our alienation from the natural world—are meant to entertain only in superficial ways. But gardening is different.

Caring too much for plants has always implied a stigma. Books like Janet Slingerland's *The Secret Lives of Plants* (2012) and films like *The Kirlian Witness* (1978) have only strengthened the idea that being too close to plants entails some kind of mental illness. The shadow of the misanthrope looms large over those who'd rather spend time in the company of plants, or pets, than busying with other humans on whatever activity is deemed normal.

The ghost of the "crazy cat lady" haunts plant lovers too—the newly coined "crazy plant lady" moniker is now emblazoned across sweaters, hats, and totes on Etsy. It's another gender-based, derogative appellation that implicitly degrades women as mad and men who love plants as women—the overarching message that being a woman is closely linked to irrationality is a vicious patriarchal ploy we know far too well.

But in truth, anthropocentrism and madness are two sides of the same coin. According to Foucault, madness does not exist as its own entity separate from reason; reason and unreason cannot escape their inherent codependency. His controversial history of madness begins with medieval practices of confinement that separated the deemed normal from the abnormal. It followed that the dehumanization of the mad in Western history became intrinsically linked to a process of animalization.

> Madness borrowed its face from the mask of the beast. Those
> chained to the cell walls were no longer men whose minds
> had wandered, but beasts preyed upon by a natural frenzy:
> as if madness, at its extreme point, freed from that moral
> unreason in which its most attenuated forms are enclosed,
> managed to rejoin, by a paroxysm of strength, the immediate
> violence of animality. This model of animality prevailed in
> the asylums and gave them their cagelike aspect, their look
> of the menagerie.[21]

This process of animalization was substantiated by capitalist notions of productivity and functionalism, or lack of thereof. The
madness of individuals was measured by the degree to which they
might no longer function in society, their divergent minds—posing
a threat to the rationalization of a society geared to fulfill capitalist demands—marginalized and repressed. Spending one's own
time caring for plants and tending to gardens (especially those
that do not yield food) is frowned on simply because it implicitly taps into a capitalist genealogy that separates the "good and
proper productivity" from the fruitless madness of the insane.
Underneath all this, the only madness at play truly is that of anthropocentrism: its relentless need to purge the nonhuman from
the human—ultimately turning the human into an unempathic,
alienated, hollow husk.

Gardening and caring for plants can be a form of political resistance to a capitalist-cultural system that wants us to care
about nature only as a resource or recreation. Between the two,
gardening can flicker with the unsettling power of a revolution.
Too much empathy for the natural world might interfere with
the primacy of capitalist exploitative needs. *Estado Vegetal* comes
back to mind. This conflict is visible across the play in the expressive power of the polyvocal dialogues, the circularities, the repetitions, the idiosyncratic expressions of the locals who sound
confused and distraught as juxtaposed to the provincial and yet
firm tone of those in power, such as the police officer. It is no co-
incidence that María Soledad, a "differently able" young woman
who has climbed up a tree in protest in the early stages of the play,
should be the most empathic voice. Her diversity is a bridge to
the nonhuman other that those who consider themselves normal

lack. How much should one care? How much empathy is too much? These are the implicit questions that *Estado Vegetal* raises from the very beginning.

Stephen King aptly explores the slippery slope between care and madness in his 1987 thriller *Misery,*[22] in which, following a car crash, romance novelist Paul Sheldon is kept captive by rescuer Annie Wilkes—his number one fan. In the story, former nurse and serial killer Wilkes is distraught by the news that in his last novel, Sheldon kills off her favorite literary character: the protagonist, Misery Chastain. Wilkes subjects the author to a series of physical and psychological tortures to coax him into rewriting an ending in which Misery survives. Wilkes nurtures deeper feelings of empathy for a fictional character than for the human author she idolizes and yet intentionally tortures. The plot quickly escalates into the horrific. Faced with relentless refusal, Wilkes amputates Sheldon's left foot to end his attempts to escape. Throughout, Wilkes's characterial emotional range unsettlingly flickers between the sweetness of a good Samaritan and the cruelty of true derangedness. Wilkes cares as deeply as her care is misdirected. This initially seems downright frightening. And yet, as Andy Warhol well expressed through his multiple multichromatic silk screens of Marilyn, Elvis, and Liz Taylor, and as Plato already knew, humans have a distinctive propensity to misdirect their care and to strongly empathize, not with the true pain of others, but with fictional characters. Rock stars and film stars disproportionately absorb the energies and efforts of teens. Despite having become an accepted cliché in popular culture since the scenes of collective euphoria triggered by the Beatles and the Rolling Stones in the 1960s, this is a relatively new phenomenon that one day might be theorized as a key phase in a new stage of capitalistic alienation that we have yet to fully understand. Ultimately, normalization is key. Any form of alienation can be normalized, as long as it fulfills some kind of capitalist demand. As Foucault demonstrates, madness is a matter of consensus and confinement. These values shift in time from one episteme to the next. Whereas violent and socially threatening individuals might more stably be classified as mad across time, the mid-range and fringes are more fluid.

Violence and the Detrimental Outcomes of Love

How much should one care? How much empathy is too much? What is rational and what is madness as, after two days of intense garden dismantling, one finds oneself, shovel in hand, digging out of the soil more than a hundred bulbs of elephant ear *(Colocasia)* on a cold October day because letting them die in the frozen ground simply isn't an option? The dismantling of the garden is as knackering as it is violent. Depending on weather conditions, gardening books advise letting a mild frost wither the large elephant ear leaves before cutting back the stems and uprooting the bulbs. The cold temperatures let the bulbs know it's time to go dormant—a condition they can withstand for many months. Sometimes, first frost and work schedule miraculously align; at other times, they don't.

Last year, I had to hack down a gloriously lush thicket of six-foot-tall elephant ears due to work schedule complications. I took a long, hard look. Asked for forgiveness. And picked up the long knife. Tears in my eyes, I cut and crushed, ripped and pulled. By the end, the gorgeous foliage was reduced to a pile of chopped-up body parts. The day had turned dark and colder. I hosed the bulbs down, wondering how the plants might have perceived what to me was traumatic. They might have registered that a major change had taken place, because plant neurobiology tells us that they can sense being touched or cut. Did they know already, or were they going to find out? Where would that knowledge reside? Language crumbles as one attempts to make sense of the subjectivity involved. All is speculative, but despite my comprehending, this something cannot be nothing for either me or them. From that point onward, and for many months, no more rain was going to drip from the pointy edges of their leaves.

But this was only half the process. To stop mold and rot from killing the bulbs, I had to peel the base of the leaves—one by one, times one hundred or so. The rubbery texture had something fishy—dolphinlike—about it. Underneath, the peeled surfaces of the bulbs looked bright pink, as if sore. By the end of the evening, the bulbs were lined up on a blanket to dry. Everything seemed too still, a vegetal sudarium. They have remained asleep all winter. Signs of a slow awakening are beginning to show as I write. A sigh of relief.

I often find myself wondering about the detrimental results of the love we pour over our nonhuman kin—their limited agency and our well-meaning, and yet often misplaced, care, resulting in unnecessary deaths or extended, involuntary torture. This flickering of the rationality of care and the madness intrinsic to our impossibility of accessing the otherness of the nonhuman is the very epistemological engine at work in *Estado Vegetal*. It is the instability of the precarious liminality between so-called sanity and madness that propels the polyvocal narratives into an epic upturning of cultural normativity—an unfolding that presents itself through at times sinister, curious, downright dark and haunting imagery that questions the boundaries of sanity and madness in our relationship with plants.

As I mentioned earlier, no other sequence in *Estado Vegetal* embodies the ethical conundrums that I have considered in relation to my relationship with plants as much as the one in which Nora, one of the elderly characters vocalized by Salinas, engages in an impromptu conversation with her potted plants. An innocent series of thought-aloud considerations about repotting her plants leads one of her vegetal kin to quip back. "What do you mean I'm not understanding your problem," Nora is heard replying, ". . . of space? That's what I'm saying. No! Don't shout at me, darling, I have my device turned on."[23] The plant's proposal turns out to be quite radical: to lift the floorboards so that the plants can return to living in the ground beneath the house. "But why would you want me to tear up the floor of my house? What do you mean, it's not my house? What do you mean, you were here before me?" The aftermath of the conversation is recounted by Joselino, a boy who regularly helps Nora with her plant care. He recalls how he found her with "her legs buried in the ground, like this, up to the height of her thigh, more or less. She was buried like . . . right there in the earth, sir! She had raised all the floorboards like . . . she had taken all the plants of the house, and I am talking about a huge number of plants, sir!" Joselino continues:

There was a tower of flowerpots, in a corner. I remember clearly that I thought the plants had kind of rebelled against the pots. You see, flowerpots were an invention of humans to do what they will, and move . . . how could I say . . . the immovable, you see; there's a reason plants grow roots, you know.[24]

The sequence ends with Joselino's bone-chilling recollection of Nora planted knee deep into the ground beneath her house, surrounded by her plants—her clothes ripped, her nails pulled back by her effort, wounded and hair tangled. Ever since, Nora's house has been repossessed by the plants. "The plants ate up the house, it's all covered up. The vines covered the doors, you can't enter or leave anymore. The house is barely visible."[25]

After positioning the last potted plant in the basement, exhausted—my feet wet and cold—I take a step back. The plants have eaten up my basement. It is now theirs. There is no room to do anything else there but water and mist them. Pots might be a human invention designed to let us move plants at will, but as I stare at them all, perched on shelves, cozying up on workbenches and stools, enjoying the heating and grow lights as temperatures outside plummet, I begin to suspect that pots might be less of a torture device and more of a vessel of care. Plants have their ways of making humans care for them. They have succeeded with so many of us for so long. The endless Instagram and Facebook plant lovers' groups sharing pictures of their phyto-lovers remind us that plants have also conquered the internet. We like to think we are the ones in charge, but plant agency unravels in subtle ways— plants play the long game like no other beings on this planet. Ultimately, that's what their lives are truly about—time.

As Michael Pollan has suggested in relation to agricultural processes, it is the crops that have domesticated us, not the other way around.[26] Our anthropocentric blinkeredness has led us to believe the opposite. We are delusional. Plants' evolutionary drive to fill every inhabitable cranny and nook of this planet doesn't stop with the limited reach of their roots or the aerial dispersal strategies of their seeds. Their ability to seduce animals and profit from their services is well known to science—orchids posing as female bees; tasty fruits; sweet nectar, fragrant blooms, and dazzling colors. We are not immune either. Plants are crafty. After all, they have been on this planet the longest. They know us well, and they know how to manipulate us to ensure their survival. My plants can't crawl, but they have made their way into my basement. They have convinced me to keep them warm and wet and to provide everything else they need. Some make it all the way into the living room and the kitchen too. They have trained me to care and

Giovanni Aloi, *Garden*, 2020.

to have their best interests at heart, sometimes at the expense of mine. But mine is now theirs, indissoluble.

As I look at my *Agave tequilana* (native to Mexico) basking under the glow of the grow lights during the Chicago winter, I understand the master plan. Suddenly, madness and sanity seem wholly inadequate terms in the context of the complex coevolutional symbioses at play in human–plant relations. Their anthropocentric roots are too shallow to reach deep enough into the layers of intricacy that can emerge only when we begin to acknowledge the rich kind of vegetal agency that, for too long, we have been taught to ignore.

Notes

1. See Richard Karban, *Plant Sensing and Communication* (Amsterdam: Amsterdam University Press, 2015); Daniel Chamovitz, *What a Plant Knows: A Field Guide to the Senses,* updated and expanded ed. (New York: Scientific American/Farrar, Straus, and Giroux, 2017); Stefano Mancuso, *The Revolutionary Genius of Plants: A New Understanding of Plant Intelligence and Behavior* (New York: Atria Books, 2018); Monica Gagliano, *Thus Spoke the Plant: A Remarkable Journey of Groundbreaking Scientific Discoveries and Personal Encounters with Plants* (Berkeley, Calif.: North Atlantic Books, 2018).

2. Manuela Infante, *Estado Vegetal,* performed at Museum of Contemporary Art Chicago, May 12, 2019, https://mcachicago.org/Calendar/2019/05/Manuela-Infante-Estado-Vegetal.

3. Catherine Horwood, *Potted History: How Houseplants Took Over Our Homes* (San Diego, Calif.: Pimpernel Press, 2021), 1.

4. Giovanni Aloi, *Why Look at Plants? The Botanical Emergence in Contemporary Art* (Leiden, Netherlands: Brill, 2018).

5. Aloi, 1.

6. Giovanni Aloi, *Lucian Freud Herbarium* (Munich: Prestel, 2019).

7. Marcel Proust, *Remembrance of Things Past* (London: Penguin Books, 2018).

8. Robin Wall Kimmerer, *Braiding Sweetgrass: Indigenous Wisdom, Scientific Knowledge and the Teachings of Plants* (Minneapolis, Minn.: Milkweed, 2013), 341.

9. Gilles Deleuze, Félix Guattari, and Robert Brinkley, "What Is a Minor Literature?," *Mississippi Review* 11, no. 3 (1983): 16.

10. Deleuze et al., 18.

11. Deleuze et al., 13.

12. Michel Foucault, *Discipline and Punish* (New York: Knopf Doubleday, 1975), 200.

13. Michel Foucault, *The Order of Things* (London: Routledge, 1966), 9.

14. Foucault, 141.

15. Foucault, 193.

16. Foucault, 143.

17. Foucault, 147.

18. Foucault.

19. Foucault.

20. The term *plant blindness* is used in the context pioneered by James H. Wandersee and Elisabeth E. Schussler, "Preventing Plant Blindness," *American Biology Teacher* 61, no. 2 (1999): 82, 84, 86.

21. Michel Foucault, *Madness and Civilization: A History of Insanity in the Age of Reason* (New York: Knopf Doubleday, 1961), 72.

22. Stephen King, *Misery* (New York: Viking Press, 1987).

23. Infante, *Estado Vegetal.*

24. Infante.

25. Infante.

26. Michael Pollan, "When a Crop Becomes King," *New York Times,* July 19, 2002, https://michaelpollan.com/articles-archive/when-a-crop -becomes-king/.

Manuela Infante and Marcela Salinas, *Estado Vegetal,* 2019. Photograph by Carmina Infante Güell. Copyright Manuela Infante.

Attending to "Plantness" in *Estado Vegetal*

Dawn Sanders

> Being human no longer determines the limits of those
> occupying the world. More than ever, these occupants
> include a number of artifacts and all living, organic and
> vegetal species.
>
> —Achille Mbembe, *Necropolitics*

In contemporary urban life, the intricate morphologies and behaviors plants display are often reduced to simple, anthropocentric, functional categories like "houseplant," "street tree," and
"food." These categories speak little of the extensive contributions
plants make to the ecological fabric of life on earth; neither do
they recognize the complex sociobiological systems within which
they live. Hence the educational task I describe in my essay "On
Trying to Understand 'Life as Plant'"[1] becomes ever more critical in a world in which many species are struggling to exist and
plants are often absent from societal view.[2]

This chapter is written from the perspective of a biology educator seeking to instill students' considerations on *life as plant* by
working in the epistemic borderlands between art and science. A
photograph from the work of Swedish graphic artist Sara Dunker
informs this educational work. It constitutes a symbol of our contemporary urban relationship with plants—how invisible plants
have become in modern society. It is the photograph of an abandoned houseplant, in a mangled plastic bag printed with a person's face, dumped on a roadside curb. This discarded, half-dead
plant, roots wrapped in a human-made material that is increasingly problematic for the living world,[3] is, in many ways, a symbol
of modern consumption.

In response to this specter of botanical loss and abandonment,

Manuela Infante's *Estado Vegetal* choreographs the human act of planting and caring for plants in a "relational space between human and plant, between the seeing and the seen," in which "there is conflict, confinement, restraint and capture."[4] But in these relational spaces are also critical moments in which the human characters, as Laurel McLaughlin states,

> appear mute alongside the plants that glacially shift into the foreground throughout the play. Willed of their own accords, they shoot off into vocal discontinuities, until the motorcyclist's admission of "I can't move" in a vegetative state reverses all roles. The vines of a peripheral chorus instead present themselves on centre stage as both protagonist and audience. A literal and clapping plant audience unveiled behind a scrim via light at the end of the play spotlights the fact that we humans have never been the primary characters.[5]

Concerning research approaches, plants—existing in the cracks and crevices of cities—are being attended to through multiple inquiry transects; as Matthew Gandy and Sandra Jaspar have observed, "the range of aesthetic and methodological questions engendered by everyday encounters with spontaneous vegetation cuts across a series of disciplinary boundaries."[6] Cities afford counterpoints between abandoned dereliction and "controlled spaces of modernity."[7] In addition to the species that survive, and thrive, within these layers of concrete, and their ruptured boundaries, a critical place for attending to plant life is exposed: the interior of the urban human home and its local environs. *Estado Vegetal* foregrounds the complexity of this multispecies site through a theatrical lens.

Despite plants' dominance in the earth's biomass and the essential role they play in perpetuating life on the planet,[8] the current status of plant life is grim. Burgeoning extinction numbers, forest fires, drought, and increased flooding due to climate change; the illegal plant trade; the clearing of ancient woodlands and forests for buildings, railways, and roads; and the continued dominance of plantation models for mass production are all active threats to plants in today's world.[9] Plant life is being brutally compromised by much of contemporary humanity's needs. The biocultural spaces plants occupy—whether circulated as amputated parts for human consumption, destabilized by climate change, or demolished for political expediency when old and too expensive to maintain—are highly political.

Estado Vegetal recognizes this sociopolitical dimension and offers us a performance in which these desecrated plant-human relations can be replaced by a question, drawn from Natasha Myers: "What might be possible if we were to alter the conditions of possibility for what we can see, say, imagine, feel and know?"[10] This, then, is theatre that speaks to philosopher Karen Houle's concern that humans should seek not to subject plants to "terms of resemblance" anchored by "the human"[11] but rather to engage with their "plantness"[12] through, in this case, a vegetal choreography of plant and human forms.

Thus, in Infante's writing and Salinas's acting, plants and humans face each other and, eventually, become entangled in one another's lives in ways that mirror the modular growth of plants. In this coming together of humans and plants, the performance addresses Michael Marder's question, what if we were to start our stories with a more plant-centric narrative; where might that take human perspectives on the vegetal?[13] In doing so, as Lucy Cotter affirms, "*Estado Vegetal* is not a plea for conservation . . . but a quietly subversive politicization of plant life, grounded in a post-Haraway conception of nature-culture."[14]

Becoming Plant in a Human Body

To grant the vegetal multiple forms and voices in *Estado Vegetal*, Infante invites the audience into a world in which plants and humans communicate and, in the case of the old woman's potted plants, request positions that take them nearer to "unrestrained growth." The notions of "unrestrained growth" and the tree "not restraining itself" are recurrent themes in the performance, exemplified by the statement "it will take plants only three months to cover everything." Such rampant plant growth is not biologically uncommon in some tropical and temperate climate species; example groups—with the capacity to grow quickly and fill space—include bamboos and brambles. But when presented in the context of *Estado Vegetal*, "unrestrained growth" takes on

Photograph by Sara Dunker. Reprinted with permission.

a different character and could be seen to symbolize a possible future—a future in which plants flourish without human oppression. However, Infante is clear that *Estado Vegetal* does not suggest that "in the era of human dominance, plants need to be saved by *us*. And it's not that if *we* are extinguished, there will be an era of plant dominance. Rather, it's that one must acknowledge that plants and humans have always been in this together, have always been enfolded into each other, but still are not the same."[15] This "enfolded together" but "not the same" message is also critical to educators seeking to engage their students with the complexity and integration of plants in ecological systems, biodiversity, plant–animal relationships, and energy flow. I believe that *Estado Vegetal* can form the core part of a biology teacher's range of representations in the classroom aimed at confronting students with the notion that plants *are* intrinsic to life.

But how can this be productively approached?

Many of the researched tensions in human perceptions of plants pertain to the otherness of their being, particularly the sessile and modular forms of plants and their ability to trap and convert light energy. *Estado Vegetal* engages with this fixity through a human–plant interface anchored by the words "I can't move," which expresses the double meaning of vegetative state for human and plant, as Manuela Infante notes in a recent interview with Laurel McLaughlin:

So, we do treat the plants as things that are not moving; and then in other moments, we treat the body of the actress as something that's not moving. For instance, all of the action is happening in the middle of the stage. This is something that you don't do in theatre—it's very "wrong." We are taught action must be evenly distributed on the stage. This notion is a very human and animal premise, that we need to use the space and profit from it. But Salinas is not migrating; she's using the centre. This is something that I did to imitate the sessility of the plant. And to confront us with our bias towards that sessility. These kinds of strategies are in place to question the idea we have of the hierarchy of that which is, to take us back to Aristotle, and the presumption that we are "animated," or ensouled.[16]

Once seeds have germinated, plants are fixed to those spots by roots, but the roots will grow, sometimes extensively, depending on species, scale, and maturity, and these roots will form numerous networks with fungi.[17] Furthermore, leaves will move in relation to sunlight—the provider of energy to the plant through the biochemical process known as photosynthesis. Toward the end of the first third of *Estado Vegetal,* the lighting is reduced to a single spotlight illuminating the face of Marcela Salinas moving as if she were a sunflower turning to the sun. Infante notes, "We wanted the actress to follow the light and not the other way around. And we started working with this in a strict way in the show. She never moves unless the light indicates that she has to turn around or to show where she's going. These are kind of laws that become invisible."[18] In these moments, the lighting itself could be understood as a second actor: sunlight, that abiotic factor so critical to the life cycle of green plants and the perpetuation of earthly life, splayed across a human face momentarily mimicking a plant's movements toward the light. The human *must* follow the light, just as the plant does. Here, then, is a moment in which plant and human movements are entangled. This moment, for an educator, is critical; slowed down, Salinas can be seen as a human proxy for a plant responding to light and, as such, can aid a more embodied approach to the concept of photosynthesis and a more sophisticated approach to plant movement—that of different time zones.[19] This is a pedagogical experience in which the biology educator, and her students, can "become plants" responding to sunlight, mirroring Salinas's theatrical bodywork. These moments of becoming plant might then be verbally unpacked in relation to questions concerning what is going on *inside* the plant. Thus we can move between drama and science to co-construct an educative experience oriented in physical, chemical, and biological processes—a process that is highly complex and one in which students, and teachers, often find themselves challenged.[20]

Throughout the performance are junctures at which the viewer is not quite sure if what one is witnessing is a human interacting with a plant or a human becoming plant. I see parallels with Han Kang's story *The Vegetarian,* as the main female character, Yeong-hye, aspires to become more "plantlike" through, first, not eating meat. Toward the end of the book, when Yeong-hye is in the hospital owing to a continued lack of nutrition, she makes the statement, "I'm not an animal anymore, sister. . . . I don't need to eat. Not now. I can live without it. All I need is sunlight." Her sister replies, "What are you talking about? Do you really think you have turned into a tree? How could a plant talk?"[21] Rose Casey has defined Yeong-hye's transition in *The Vegetarian* as "willed arboreality."[22] One could imagine similar terms being applied to critical moments in *Estado Vegetal* when Salinas forces her body to hold and contain vegetal being while facing the light—her source of energy in her physical rendition of "plantness." In so doing, Salinas retracts her mobile animated human presence, like a snail withdrawing its tentacles, and immediately slows down into her alternative vegetal state. The contrasting states she presents function as borderlands between the highly animated human and the seemingly restrained plant. Over time, this changes, and both become increasingly enfolded and intertwined with the other in a choreography of beings, just as plants are deeply entwined within human life, if, albeit, often deemed invisible.[23] Watching Salinas choreograph human/plant characters is an educational resource for biology teachers seeking to open up conversations concerning biological similarities and differences between plants and humans, as well as an opportunity to ask questions about the ways in which plant and human lives coalesce. It also provokes a challenge for biology educators: how are we using our own bodies in representations of "plantness" in our teaching, and do we create embodied experiences with our students?

Time, Ghost Houses, and Jungles

Elements of human and plant time surround the ghost houses and plant-filled jungles that entangle the human characters in *Estado Vegetal*. Performance in this context is used as an imaginary in which plants thrive and humans struggle—a reversal of the current sociobiological landscape described in the introduction of this chapter. In particular, the picture portrayed of a street tree "grown monstrously," eating up pedestrian spaces, offers fecundity in a world in which mature, long-lived trees are being denied further life; on the edges, and in the center, of forests and in urban streets, these arboreal elders are being cut, often for economic reasons. Thus *Estado Vegetal*'s opening dialogue about the tree (for example, the monologue concerning the street tree, its maintenance, and the cost) can be read as a metaphor for current struggles for plant life enveloped by time and money.

However, as the performance develops, we are taken into scenes of a more unified plant–human conversation, such as one in which an old woman's houseplants insist that their pots be moved to the ground. The woman removes the floorboards so that her plants can take root in the soil below and thus shifts her plants from a position of entrapment to possibilities of emancipated growth. As Cotter notes, "the plants' subsequent reclamation of the old woman's house, and its ultimate disappearance in a jungle of weeds, pre-empts a recurring proposition in the play that plants will reclaim the earth following the demise of human beings."[24] Such a claim mirrors Achille Mbembe's recent observation that "the terrestrial condition was never the unique lot of humans."[25] Thus, in its rawest essence, the play engages with the multispecies reality of the earth's functional biomass and the fractional part humans represent.[26] This is the vital message plant educators work to deliver in pedagogical spaces from classrooms to botanic gardens all over the world—the ecological meaning behind the concept "Plants = Life."[27]

Yet, despite the depth of "plantness" in the performance, *Estado Vegetal* contains a strange material dissonance; the plant props are plastic—mere effigies of their living counterparts. However, their greenness anchors them to their botanical identities. Their theatrical role retains the power to bring life as plant into our human perception: sound, light, nonmovement, empty space, shadows, and, of course, shades of green. This is aligned to the challenges educators face when teaching with, and about, plants and the ways in which drawing on the performance could support us to teach in a more embodied, theatrical way. Of course, this also bears implications for the spaces in which educators work and the persistence of particular arrangements of classrooms and laboratories. How might we change these pedagogical spaces if we truly are to make plants subjects rather than objects in biology education, and, as questioned earlier, where do we place our own teaching bodies in the context of this emancipatory act?

Entangled Lives as Educational Performance

Teaching about plants contains numerous obstacles well docu-
mented in biology education research.[28] Some of these obstacles
are related to the curriculum, others to the ways in which teachers choose to teach about plants, and some are related to student
perceptions of plant characteristics. Educational researchers have
begun to explore performance as a means by which to make the
private lives of plants public.[29] It is in these educational inter-
stices between biology education and performance art that *Estado
Vegetal* occupies a specific role. These dramatic provocations are
particularly apt for teachers who want to address questions that
move away from the purely biological concerns of individual form
and function to broader questions of ecological relationships and
biodiverse life, such as those represented by the plant kingdom.
As Dawn Sanders and Dan Jenkins have noted, "being rooted in
one place requires plants to develop highly sophisticated capacities to respond, communicate and react to external stimuli,
physical attack and competition with others, develop mutualistic
partnerships and, ultimately, reproduce. In addition, the ability
of plants to photosynthesize makes them a critical component in
food webs."[30] *Estado Vegetal* captures not only the social complexities of "life as plant" in the contemporary world but some biological ones too. However, this is by no means a linear narrative nor
indeed one in which the human actor should take the lead role.
The geometry of the stage set, in particular, the wooden table, is
a critical component, as a symbol of a line representing the earth
and a divide between what is visible and what is unseen and, perhaps, unknown—a world of darkness and plant roots. As Infante
observes, the table, in this context, "is used in a simple way to
imitate and trespass that border. Marcela uses her hand to cross
straight down through the table as a magician would, and then at
the end she goes straight up through the table to become a plant.
The table is a magical border."[31] Likewise, biology teachers use
various physical props and verbal analogies to bring the unknown
and unseen world of plants to the light of human attention.[32]

Hence working with plants in modern biology education is not
just a task of presenting scientific knowledge to our students, in
my case, student teachers, but also an affective act concerning the

development of values needed to see the "other" and recognize the collective ecological network that plants and humans inhabit. In working with both knowledge *and* values, biological education has increasingly become multimodal and interdisciplinary.[33] In this context, we are seeing a greater number of epistemic border crossings between art and science in both educational praxis and work in the arts.[34] From a personal perspective, underpinning this integration is a desire to increase attentional distance to plants, "the degree to which the observer attends or focuses on an object," *and* emotional distance, "the level of response that an observer maintains towards an object."[35]

Performance art like *Estado Vegetal* has a role to play in such acts of attention, for as Edwin Ulloa has observed, "*Estado Vegetal* dances tirelessly around an impossible dialogue; that of humans and plants. A failed dialogue with nature that is, perhaps, our most innate monologue."[36]

It is so that Infante's work in *Estado Vegetal* embodies the desire to make the otherness of plants present and recognized and, through its "enfolded" approach, helps us to witness plants for the complex beings they are, especially when the plants and their multivocal presence are foregrounded in the latter stages of the play. As a teacher, I have come to realize that the struggles to represent plants in my teaching are sociobiological. In mirroring the words of Judith Butler, the "you" in my work is "plants": "Though I thought I was having a relation to 'you,' I find that I am caught up in a struggle with norms. But could it also be true that I would not be in this struggle with norms if it were not for a desire to offer recognition to you?"[37] Perhaps, as educators, we might harness the performative presence of *Estado Vegetal* to facilitate embodied attentional and emotional relationships with plants and, in this educative move, afford recognition of the sociobiological depth of the "plantness" of plants and thus demobilize the rooted norms of their absent beings in much of contemporary biology education.

Notes

1. Dawn Sanders, "On Trying to Understand 'Life as Plant': Fielding Impressions of Art-Based Research Installation in a Botanic Garden," in *Beyond Plant Blindness: Seeing the Importance of Plants for a Sustainable*

World, ed. Bryndis H. Snæbjörnsdóttir, Mark Wilson, and Dawn Sanders, 40–49 (Berlin: Green Box, 2020).

2. Kathy J. Willis, ed., *State of the World's Plants Report 2017* (London: Royal Botanic Gardens Kew, 2017).

3. Emily Elhacham, Liad Ben-Uri, Jonathon Grozovski, Yinon M. Bar-On, and Ron Milo, "Global Human-Made Mass Exceeds All Living Biomass," *Nature* 588, no. 7838 (2020): 442–44.

4. Dawn Sanders, *Encounters with Conflict and Intimacy: The Presence of Plants in the Work of Ellie Kyungran Heo* (Gothenburg, Sweden: Galleri 54, 2020).

5. Laurel V. McLaughlin, "*Estado Vegetal,* a Gesture of Imitation: An Interview with Manuela Infante," *Performance Research* 25, no. 2 (2020): 30.

6. Matthew Gandy and Sandra Jaspar, *The Botanical City* (Berlin: Jovis, 2020), 11.

7. Gandy and Jaspar, 11.

8. Yinon M. Bar-On, Rob Phillips, and Ron Milo, "The Biomass Distribution on Earth," *Proceedings of the National Academy of Sciences of the United States of America* 115, no. 25 (2018): 6506–11. https://doi.org/10.1073/pnas.1711842115.

9. See, e.g., the following studies and assessment reports on the state of plants: Renato J. Orsato, Stewart R. Clegg, and Horacio Falcão, "The Political Ecology of Palm Oil Production," *Journal of Change Management* 13, no. 4 (2013): 444–59; Willis, *State of the World's Plants*; Intergovernmental Science-Policy Platform on Biodiversity and Ecosystem Services, *Global Assessment Report* (Bonn, Germany: IPBES, 2019); and Intergovernmental Panel on Climate Change, "Summary for Policymakers," in *Climate Change 2021: The Physical Science Basis. Contribution of Working Group I to the Sixth Assessment Report of the Intergovernmental Panel on Climate Change,* ed. Valérie Masson-Delmotte, Panmao Zhai, Anna Pirani, Sarah L. Connors, Clotilde Péan, Yang Chen, Leah Goldfarb et al., 3–34 (Cambridge: Cambridge University Press, 2021).

10. Natasha Myers, "Anthropologist as Transducer in a Field of Affects," in *Knowings and Knots: Methodologies and Ecologies in Research-Creation,* ed. Natalie Loveless (Edmonton: University of Alberta Press, 2020), 98.

11. Karen L. F. Houle, "Animal, Vegetable, Mineral: Ethics as Extension or Becoming? The Case of Becoming-Plant," *Journal for Critical Animal Studies* 9, no. 1/2 (2011): 89–116.

12. W. Marshall Darley, "The Essence of 'Plantness,'" *American Biology Teacher* 52, no. 6 (1990): 354–57.

13. Michael Marder, *The Chernobyl Herbarium: Fragments of an Exploded Consciousness* (London: Open Humanities Press, 2016).

14. Lucy Cotter, "Plants as Other: Manuela Infante's Estado Vegetal," *Mousse,* May 17, 2029, https://www.moussemagazine.it/magazine/manuela-infante-lucy-cotter-2019/.

15. McLaughlin, "*Estado Vegetal*," 32.
16. McLaughlin, 32.
17. Lynne Boddy, *Fungi and Trees: Their Complex Relationships* (Stonehouse, U.K.: Arboricultural Association, 2021).
18. McLaughlin, "*Estado Vegetal*," 34.
19. Dawn Sanders, "Trapped in Time: Lingering with 'Plantness,'" *Plants, People, Planet* 1 (2019): 64–66. For a deeper discussion of embodiment and plant education, see Margaretha Häggström, "*Estetiska erfarenheter i naturmöten: En fenomenologisk studie av upplevelser av skog, växtlighet och undervisning*" (doctoral thesis, Gothenburg Studies in Educational Sciences, Acta Universitatis Gothoburgensis, 2020).
20. Dawn L. Sanders and Dan Jenkins, "Plant Biology in Teaching Biology," in *Schools: Global Issues, Research and Trends,* ed. K. Kampourakis and M. J. Reiss, 124–38 (New York: Routledge, 2018).
21. Han Kang, *The Vegetarian* (London: Granta, 2015), 153–54.
22. Rose Casey, "Willed Arboreality: Feminist Worldmaking in Han Kang's *The Vegetarian*," *Critique: Studies in Contemporary Fiction* 62, no. 3 (2021): 347–60.
23. Dawn L. Sanders, "Standing in the Shadows of Plants," *Plants, People, Planet* 1 (2019): 130–38.
24. Cotter, "Plants as Other."
25. Achille Mbembe, *Necropolitics* (Durham, N.C.: Duke University Press, 2019), 184.
26. Bar-On et al., "Biomass Distribution on Earth."
27. J. Galbraith, "Connecting with Plants: Lessons for Life," *Curriculum Journal* 14, no. 2 (2003): 279–86.
28. See, e.g., Howard Thomas, Helen Ougham, and Dawn Sanders, "Plant Blindness and Sustainability," *International Journal of Sustainability in Higher Education* 23, no. 1 (2022): 41–57.
29. See, e.g., Bethan C. Stagg and Michael F. Verde, "Story of a Seed: Educational Theatre Improves Students' Comprehension of Plant Reproduction and Attitudes to Plants in Primary Science Education," *Research in Science and Technological Education* 37, no. 1 (2019): 15–35.
30. Sanders and Jenkins, "Plant Biology in Teaching Biology," 128.
31. McLaughlin, "*Estado Vegetal*."
32. Sanders and Jenkins, "Plant Biology in Teaching Biology."
33. E.g., Dawn Sanders, "Reflecting on Boundary Crossings between Knowledge and Values: A Place for Multimodal Objects in Biology Didactics?," *Nordic Studies in Science Education* 18, no. 2 (2022): 214–24.
34. See, e.g., Giovanni Aloi, *Lucian Freud Herbarium* (Munich: Prestel, 2019); Laura Colucci-Gray and Pamela Burnard, *Why Science and Art Creativities Matter: (Re-)configuring STEAM for Future-making Education* (Leiden, Netherlands: Brill, 2020).

35. Shifra Schonmann, *Theatre as a Medium for Children and Young People: Images and Observations* (Cham, Switzerland: Springer, 2006), 66.

36. Cuban Theater Digital Archive, http://ctda.library.miami.edu /production/5410.

37. Judith Butler, *Giving an Account of Oneself* (New York: Fordham University Press, 2005).

Manuela Infante and Marcela Salinas, *Estado Vegetal*, 2019. Photograph by Miguel Lecaros. Copyright Manuela Infante.

"I Can't Move"
Plants and the Politics of Mobility in *Estado Vegetal*

Catriona Sandilands and Prudence Gibson

In the opening scene of *Estado Vegetal,* actor Marcela Salinas stands at a microphone as the character Don Raúl, a worker "in charge of green spaces." Don Raúl is under question about a tree in his jurisdiction that has become a matter of concern because of a motorcycle accident in which a young man, Manuel, crashed into it. The motorcyclist remains in hospital in a vegetative state. The tree has been controversial for some time. A neighbor, Eva, has complained about its "excessive" and "unrestrained growth" into the power lines so often that council has agreed to cut it back. A young woman, María Soledad, has taken to sitting in the tree in protest; she has to be dragged down on several occasions. When asked by Don Raúl if she saw anything the day of the accident, María Soledad says the tree "had fallen asleep" despite its moving leaves. She also tells him she heard the tree sound like a chorus of many voices, "oh, no, we won't go."

This scene introduces many key themes in the play. For this essay, it draws particular attention to questions of vegetal *movement and unmovement.* For Manuel, the immobility of the tree brings about his undoing; for Eva, its unruly growth signals menace; for María Soledad, its rhythms are part of her intimate knowledge of it, and its voice inspires her to join in its declaration of the right to be stationary. But Don Raúl sums it up:

> The thing is, you don't see a tree move. Because what happens? A tree moves so slowly that it seems still. A tree lives for . . . how long? Hundreds of years! So then, of course, imagine your life, your very own life, stretched out to hundreds of years SLOW.

So then, of course . . . you could say "you should have seen it coming, Don Raúl," "the storm was approaching, Don Raúl," but I would have to answer: "Yes, officer, but YOU COULD NOT SEE IT." That's the central issue in all of this: this is a COMING that CANNOT BE SEEN.[1]

This tree speaks eloquently about mobility and its place in registers of animacy, temporality, and modes of (be)coming. Plants *do* move, through growth, in evolutionary and vegetal time, by interfering with power lines, by rustling in the wind. But plants also *refuse* to move and, indeed, often find their genius loci in behaviors that are rooted in place and that are often threatened by human fixations with speed. *Estado Vegetal* plays with these ideas about mobility and performs a complex interrogation of movement as a mark of animacy; in particular, it prompts us to think about the relationship between movement and futurity and to contrast forward linear progress with vegetal time and change. Furthermore, the performance of plant movement and unmovement in *Estado Vegetal* is profoundly gendered: compare, for example, Manuel's motorcycle with María Soledad's tree-sitting. Our reading of the play is, then, oriented to understanding how *Estado Vegetal* inspires an ecofeminist line of questioning around plants and the gendered politics of speed and movement.

"I Can't Move": *Estado Vegetal*'s Movements and Unmovements

There is so much movement and unmovement in *Estado Vegetal*! After the opening scene, the spotlight focuses on Eva, who tells the story of the crash: that she was sleeping, "perfectly still," that the power went off with a boom, that she went outside and saw pieces of body and motorbike in the street, and that she encountered a broken Manuel with the question "where are your legs?" to which he responded, "I can't move." Eva describes the tree and its movements prior to the accident: it was "eating up the pedestrians' space" and would, eventually, "walk away on its own." She introduces us to a larger movement of plants, in the "ghost house" on the street, which the plants have "swallowed," like in the TV show where "human beings are no longer on the face of the earth" and "it will take plants only three months to cover everything." And then she describes Manuel's mother at the police station: she "caught my attention because I saw her, I saw her so undaunted, so immovable, just like . . . planted there."

The spotlight rises on Manuel's mother, who describes her experience of her son's overwhelming desire to move. When he was a child, she enrolled him in recreational programs because he couldn't stay still. He refused to play the part of a tree in a school play because he couldn't move in the costume. When he became an adult, he "was always running against time" and "because of all that coming and going, he would forget things." He always wanted "to be somewhere else." Manuel becomes a firefighter, and "even this . . . was because of this issue of speed."

The scene shifts to an old woman, years earlier, in the "ghost house." She addresses one of the potted plants, and the plant talks back to her in a way that she clearly comprehends; the conversation is all about movement. He tells her the plants need to move beyond pots; he accuses her of running off when she doesn't understand that what they want is the freedom to move of their own accord, requiring that she lift the floorboards so they can root into the earth below the house. When she doesn't perform the task quickly enough, she replies, "I'm going as fast as I can, honey."[2] By the time her helper, Joselino, finds them, she has taken the plants out of their pots, buried their roots in the earth underneath the house, and joined them, buried in the soil. He tells the interrogators about the discovery: "I thought the plants had . . . rebelled against the pots." Where the pots had allowed "humans to do what they will, and move . . . the immovable," the rebellion meant that the plants' roots, now in the earth, could lift "the sidewalk of the whole block" and move "all the way to the roots of the tree at issue."[3] "They are up to something," he says to the interrogators: "this is such a slow coming that you don't see it."

The next scene performs a poem the plants have dictated to the old woman. When retrieved by Joselino, it is just a dry leaf that crackles like the sound of a fire. The crackling crescendos into a wildfire to which a firefighter (Manuel) responds, and on which he reflects. This climactic scene involves a soliloquy in which Manuel confesses to the burning trees his animal guilt about his relationship to movement, and the role of this movement in their immolation: "You live within time, not against it. I am animal. My response to the world was to flee, my condemnation, then, was movement. When you stay, I move forward. Where you settle, I evade. In the face of difficulty, I avoid. Where you establish, I invade." He names the relationship between animal movement and the idea of progress, speeding forward, which he contrasts to plant cyclicity: "May death be something that occurs in my chest, while my back, in turn, is born, so I never get the absurd idea that we are moving forward."

In the final scene, Manuel's mother enters the spotlight again. She receives the interrogators' judgment on the accident, and now the judges are the plants. They offer her scant solace for her son's vegetative state: in rendering him immobile, the tree simply brought Manuel into "his kingdom." She wants answers: "Why so much moving here and there?" "How does something that can't move live?" "Do you know why the tree could have killed Manuel and not Manuel the tree?" The answers boil down to one thing: people are obsessed with movement, trees know their places, and "the stiller something is, the more it survives." Where the opening scene raises the absurd possibility that the tree *caused* the accident, the closing scene confirms that it did. Not only is the tree "the culprit" but the overall stillness and non-forward movement of plants is their world-making "plot": as they took over the ghost house and later the street, they will, as in the TV show, eventually take over everything, enfolding necrophilic speed into a much slower sort of movement, a "coming that cannot be seen."

In this unfolding, the play performs a contrast between plant and human movement to develop a specifically vegetal critique of the fast and fatal modernity that caused Manuel to move compulsively from place to place, putting out one fire after another. Manuel's obsession with movement kills him; this same genre of movement is also the cause of the catastrophic wildfire that inspires his dramatic apology. Plants, in contrast, are not rapid, not linear, not obsessive, but eventually more powerful. Their movements are cyclical, spreading, rooting; indeed, their temporalities are ancient, and we humans are, despite our accelerated hubris, a mere blip in the midst of their planetary emergence.

Estado Vegetal also highlights that people can have some access to this vegetative experience of rootedness and lull. Of course, there is Manuel, whose unwilling experience of vegetal stillness after the accident is a horrific response to his apology for his animal movement. The old woman, too, experiences harm as she buries herself in the soil: even though she is slow enough to hear the plants talk, she cannot physically become one herself. But then there is the experience of sleep: Eva "was perfectly still" before the accident, and Manuel "sleeps like a log." And then there is Manuel's mother, who, at the police station, is so unmoving that she looks to Eva like she was "planted there." Perhaps most importantly, there is María Soledad, for whom the cry "I can't move" is about refusal, not inability: her determination to stay put against the firemen is a form of arboreal solidarity emphasized by her blending into the chorus of plants, *"no me puedo mover."*

These experiences of movement and stillness are strongly gendered, and *Estado Vegetal* should be viewed as a rich work of *ecofeminist* performance. Its feminist angle is sophisticated. Women do not have an essential, inherent "connection" to the temporalities and movements of plants; indeed, Eva is the most arborophobic character of all, and the old woman dies because she takes her plant relationships too far. However, some of the characters find themselves in intimate circumstances in which their lives are stilled enough to be able to listen to vegetal rhythms, to imagine their own corporeal involvements in plant temporalities and movements.

In addition, the play itself moves vegetally, creating an *experience* of narrative growth and development that is accretive rather than linear. Phrases and images are repeated by different characters in different scenes: "I can't move," "a coming that cannot be seen," "how can something that can't move live?" This repetition is amplified by Salinas playing all the parts and by the play's use of audio recordings to create onstage conversations with herself in different roles at the same time. The plot moves fluidly from present to past to future in a plural unfolding involving the entwined lives of many people and plants. The earliest scene chronologically (with the old woman) is in the middle of the play and emerges into the present by way of an older Joselino's memory, but the plants have already arrived at the tree before the play even begins. Finally, the scene in which Manuel's mother describes his life narratively loops around itself: she presents part of an image,

moves on, comes back to it with more detail, and only completes
the story at the very end of the scene. The energy of the play's
movement, throughout, goes in cycles, and the story is a literal
entanglement of lives, temporalities, and speeds, both plant and
human.

"A Coming That Cannot Be Seen"?
Movement as Plant Desire

Plant movements are often imperceptible. Much vegetal movement occurs at night when humans sleep or it is too dark to observe. Plant movement often progresses in a slower time frame
that is not obvious within limited, anthropocentric understandings of time and scale. Plants nevertheless move, sometimes vig-
orously: they turn by day and curl by night; they stretch to the sun
and close against frost; they shift and change to accept raindrops.
Yet all that most humans see is the bend of a tree in the wind,
the wave of grasses in a breeze. Could human ignorance about
plant movement be explained by a deep mortal fear of imminent
human decline (and irrelevance) or by a deeper androcentric fear
of women's potential to move, excessively? If humans accept that
plants move, really move, in ways humans don't understand, then
will that new knowledge stop us in our tracks?

In addition to an improved human comprehension of the ani-
mistic and independent movement of plants, a better realization
of plant movement might throw into question all forms of human
mastery.[4] The pace of human land clearing and vegetal collecting
for economic gain has been at high speed, especially during colonial periods. These practices have been effective in curtailing and
oppressing the wildly and excessively vegetal, in ways that also
bear witness to (attempted) mastery over First Nations people and
women.[5]

Estado Vegetal is an experiment in this theme of movement
against mastery. It presents in part as a cautionary tale: if we
allow houseplants to take over the floor, we will need to be dug
free; if we start listening to the communications of trees instead
of each other, there will be fatal accidents; if human acceleration-
ism is speeding humans toward the future, it will lead to a pre-
mature decline. And yet, viewers of the play get the sense that

the real caution is not the threat of plants but the adverse legacy of human betrayal and, particularly, the gendered disavowal of women and concomitant denial of responsibility for plants.[6]

While some scholars have written against the conception of plants as unmoving, such as Dov Koller's work on restless plants, it is in fact the paradox of human perception of plants as undynamic, when they are very dynamic, that allows an ecofeminist reading of freedom as being both moving and not moving.[7] Ecofeminism understands that all oppressions occur together (of Indigenous people, of women, of nature); as a result, new knowledge of the mobile and excessive characteristics of plants has the capacity to trigger a wide-eyed awareness of the power of other overlooked entities, alongside plants. An understanding that being still can be more powerful than purposeful striving accentuates how both plants and women are allied objects of male fear, unless their movement is curtailed. While several of Infante's characters cannot move, the meaning of their immobility differs: being fixed in one place, being politically determined to sit in, and being oppressed against one's own will of movement are not the same, and they are also not mutually exclusive. A lack of movement has connotations of mastery and oppression, but also of allure and strength. This paradox sits at the heart of the play, and it is steeped in ecofeminist observations of women, people of color, and "nature" as dominated, constrained, and controlled in their movements.[8]

Estado Vegetal also draws on histories of plant movement knowledge. Greek philosopher Theophrastus and naturalist Charles Darwin remain key figures in the study of plant movement. Although much of their work is observational and lacks the technological and cellular details of contemporary science, it nevertheless addresses the secret movements of plants, as unseen by the average human. As a result, it foreshadows Infante's awareness of plants' capacities to move. Theophrastus's *Enquiry into Plants* was written in approximately 350–280 B.C. and included observation-based writing on the rate of growth of trees and the length of their roots.[9] He detailed how trees grow faster when waterside; how a tree trunk first divides, then divides again; and how growth occurs from the top of the shoots or the side buds. Just as the character María Soledad sits in the great tree and hears its voices,

Theophrastus set himself the task of spending slow time with the trees and noted that all buds end in a single leaf "wherefore it is reasonable that they should not make fresh buds and growth from that point, as they have no point of departure."[10]

More than two thousand years later, Charles Darwin's book on the movement of plants focused on their capacity to sleep.[11] Research for this tome was conducted by Darwin and his children; the book is written in first person plural, reflecting the family style of research project, and involved the repeated dragging of pots out of a greenhouse into the night for testing. Darwin tested the leaves of various plants, including especially the mimosa *(Mimosa pudica)* or "sensitive plant." Darwin aimed to give a name to the sleep movements of plants: *night-turning.* He noticed the spiral or ellipsis nocturnal movement of plants. He noticed how trifolium move at an angle of ninety degrees and that, during the night, this movement is rapid. The movement is complicated with movement vertically upward and downward. He wrote that "it is hardly possible to doubt that plants must derive some great advantage from such remarkable powers of movement."[12] The turgescence (turgid inflation) of the cells influences the amount of movement. He noted the functional importance of such movement in plants.[13]

Within the limits of Darwin's observations of plant function, it makes sense for plants to move toward the sun during daylight but away from the sky at night. Darwin thought they did it to protect their surfaces from chill. So, the sleep movements of leaves saved them from injury. Trifolium crowd their leaves together when they sleep to achieve further protection. Darwin and his family team did experiments where they did not let the plants move their leaves away from the sky. They moved the plants outside at dusk under the night, all of which "exposed the evil effects of the leaves not being allowed to assume at night their normal dependent position."[14] Their leaves tied into place, the trifolium subsequently suffered from the frost and were injured. The Darwins also tied some leaves in horizontal position, stopping them from sleeping in the vertical position, and they consequently died.

Of course, they used lots of pots in these experiments. One wonders what Infante might say about these experiments involving no soil, no ground, and extreme confinement. Still, Darwin found that it wasn't just the closing of leaves but the movement of the branches at night that prevented plant injury. Whippo argues that Darwin looked at plant movement as a way to support and defend his wider argument that plants could still acquire new behavioral traits, a complement to his theory of evolution. Infante's play seems to support Darwin's notion that acquiring "extra" plant-like behavioral traits is possible. The old woman wants to root her legs in the soil; María Soledad knows how to hear the trees' voices. Darwin also made several conclusions that have yet to be challenged, such as his observation that if plants did not get enough illumination during the day, they would not sleep at night. Despite our human perception of the "still of night," plants are moving.

Ken Thompson, in *Darwin's Most Wonderful Plants,* notes that Darwin foresaw and preempted much of the most recent groundbreaking work of plant science.[15] Indeed, Darwin's work with *M. pudica* is taken up by Monica Gagliano, who experimented with suddenly dropping the plants (via a safe apparatus), which retract their sensitive leaves when distressed. Gagliano concluded that the mimosa plants learned and remembered that each fall was not going to cause injury and duly stopped retracting their leaves.[16] This understanding that plants can learn and remember movement also informs *Estado Vegetal.*

Developments in plant science have shifted the way humans philosophize plants. Only now do we understand the inner, cellular workings of their movements. In fact, only thanks to the visualizing of plant movement has the field opened up to the riches of their mobility, as evidenced in Oliver Gaycken's work on nineteenth-century plant biologist Wilhelm Pfeffer, who made four influential time-lapse films of tulips in 1898–1900.[17] Gaycken underlines how Darwin and Pfeffer made connections between root tips and base animal brains. He also notes how time-lapse videos gave visual evidence for the vitality and mobility of plants, as they translated plant time into a speed to which human beings could pay attention.

Infante's play performs these shifts away from hierarchical, androcentric, and human-centered considerations of plant life. We now know that plants have the capacity to make decisions and communicate and, especially, to move. These capacities throw into doubt the Judeo-Christian desire to master nature, to hold dominion over plant (and all other) life. The idea that the rustling of leaves or the budding of flowers or the swaying of branches is not for human consciousness and comprehension but for the vegetal world itself is a shock to ingrained anthropocentrism. How do we make sense of plants if they are no longer just the building blocks of poetry and art, there for our delectation? For Infante, deeper undertakings of plant movement are at play, such as the discordant rate of human-to-plant growth, the accelerationist pace of human existence, the biopolitics of human–plant lives together, and the chilling new awareness that an apical human position may be self-immolating hubris.

Manuel's grieving mother mourns the kind of extreme speed of movement that she sees as the cause of her son's death. With that mourning comes a longer and deeper mourning of the immobility of women. In fact, women and plants have been aesthetically flattened together throughout the history of painting, where women and flowers, in inert domestic settings, sit on gallery walls in juxtaposition with images of men outdoors, undertaking activity and conquering nature.[18] The association of containment with the domestication of women is clear, but the containment of potted plants and cultivated gardens also sits alongside other elements of mastery in ecofeminist, decolonial understandings.[19] Movement of women and plants can be seen as a direct threat to androcentrism and anthropocentrism. But, move we do. When Infante writes of the old woman's listening to her potted plants' demands to be liberated, she sets them free. Yet the plants want more: they still feel confined due to their lack of access to soil, and the old woman is soon scrabbling and digging up her floor to set the plants truly free to grow, and to speak. The wildness of the plants is thrilling. But there is a sense of danger and fear around this unleashing of the plants. All women who have found their voice and found their freedom know exactly what that sense of danger truly feels like: it feels like the plants in the old woman's house.

"Oh, No, We Won't Go!" Unmovement as Plant Protest

María Soledad sits in the great tree and refuses to move even as the firefighters drag her down. "Oh, no, we won't go!" She allies herself with the tree's refusal and, in so doing, places herself in a storied history of other plant refusals of unwilling movement, such as tree-sitting. Although tree-sitting has multiple origins,[20] its current form as an organized political practice began in the Pureora Forest of New Zealand in 1978, in which a small group of activists lived in platforms in giant tōtara trees that were scheduled to be cut down, to make it as difficult as possible for logging to proceed in the area.[21] While tree-sitting is now more often viewed as a way of stalling the cutting of significant or strategic trees long enough to achieve a longer-term legal reprieve, in this case, the tactic was relatively successful and resulted in the establishment of Pureora Forest Park. Subsequent highly publicized, organized tree-sits have occurred in the United States, Canada, the United Kingdom, Germany, and New Zealand; they have also been organized to protest mining, road expansion, and pipeline construction as well as logging.

The ongoing story of tree-sitting can be told from many places, including Australia and Canada, from which settler-colonized places we are writing. Just this year, there were sit-ins and blockades at the Tarkine Forest in Tasmania and at Fairy Creek on Vancouver Island, British Columbia. In the Tarkine, a long line of activists have sat-in high in trees, swaying on their porta-ledges, to save the forest from logging.[22] At Fairy Creek, on traditional Pacheedaht, Ditidaht, and Huu-ay-aht territory, both settler and Indigenous protestors participated in the largest civil disobedience in Canadian history to prevent logging company Teal-Jones from clear-cutting one of the last remaining stands of old-growth timber in the region; tactics of immobility there have included tree-sits, tripods, and "sleeping dragons" that secure protestors' limbs in pipes in concrete-filled holes.[23] These stories of *politicized immobility* emphasize and amplify the power of refusing to move according to capitalist temporalities. At the same time, in their emphasis on protecting ancient trees with slow lives and long memories, they also also generate respect for plant/tree movements on their own terms.

Tree-sits are particularly effective because they perform a smart biopolitical substitution. If the life of a tree or forest on its own is not enough to stop logging or other destructive development, then a person can step in to become a life that, under the circumstances, actually *matters* enough for logging to be stopped (if the tree is cut down, the *person* will die). Both lives may be fiercely immobile, but they are not politically equivalent, and tree-sitting plays with this inequality. Furthermore, tree-sits are effective because they often involve trees that, for one reason or another, are more charismatic and therefore more likely to become "lives that matter" in their own right as a result of the tree-sitters' immobility. Perhaps the most famous example of this coming-to-matter involves Julia Butterfly Hill's relationship with Luna, a fifteen-hundred-year-old redwood in Humboldt County, California, scheduled to be clear-cut by the Pacific Logging Company (PLC). Starting in December 1997, Hill lived for 738 days on two platforms built in the tree's branches, fifty-five meters above the ground, during which time she and Luna became celebrities. In 1999, PLC agreed to preserve the tree and a small, sixty-one-meter buffer zone, but the surrounding publicity had a larger impact on public understanding of the lives, and liveliness, of trees.[24] Twenty years later, Richard Powers picked up on the intensity of Hill's and others' intimate relationships with the trees in which they sat for days, months, and years in his novel *The Overstory,* in which characters Olivia Vandergriff ("Maidenhair") and Nicholas Hoel ("Watchman") live in another giant redwood, Mimas, for over a year before it is cut down.[25] In Hill, Olivia, Nicholas, and María Soledad—and among land defenders in the Tarkine and at Fairy Creek—trees have personal witnesses, protectors, and publicists of arboreal liveliness; this palpable affinity is born from shared, resistant immobility: oh, no, we won't go.

Not all tree sitters have been women.[26] Similarly, not all feminist sitting *with* trees has involved spectacular heights or personalities. The 1970s Chipko movement in (then) Uttar Pradesh famously involved networks of village women hugging ash and other trees to place their bodies in the way of loggers' axes; they held their ground with the trees both for the trees' futures and, importantly, for their own. Claiming an intimate relationship with the trees on the basis of centuries of shared livelihood, not to mention extensive knowledge of their role in preventing flooding, drought, and erosion, the women resisted through such tactics as wrapping colored threads around the trees to emphasize the ecological and political entwinement of their ongoing interests.[27] More recently, forest ecologist Suzanne Simard sat with the trees long enough to actually hear them talking.[28] Her research on the mycorrhizal communicative and social networks involved in Douglas fir forests has had an extraordinary impact on both scholarship and popular culture; for example, her "Mother Tree" was also the inspiration for the "Home Tree" in James Cameron's 2009 film *Avatar*.[29] Feminist and other women's eco-activist groups, such as the Dirt Witches and the Climate Factory in Australia,[30] the Pocket Forests in Ireland,[31] the Friends of Clayoquot Sound in Canada,[32] women protesting pipeline expansion in U.S. Appalachia,[33] and even women "marrying" trees in the United Kingdom and Mexico,[34] were/are all engaged in acts of stillness *with* trees, forms of activism that involve slowing down to reduce the speed of extraction and industry and to draw attention to the slower, more abiding, and strongly gendered relationships and temporalities that are destroyed in the rush to cut, to re/move, and to re/place.

The thing is that all of these broadly ecofeminist actions, not to mention the long-standing and multiplying Indigenous actions around the globe, from Unist'ot'en to the Western Freeway, led by Indigenous women, are not only about immobility and refusal of capitalist time: they are also about recognizing and understanding ongoing plant movements and the involvements of people in these movements. In her account of her relationship with Luna, Hill makes a point of describing how much Luna *moved* and how challenging it was for her to stay safe, high in a tree in the middle of gale-force winds.[35] In their work to refuse oil pipeline development in Virginia, activists not only use unmovement protocols developed in Black civil rights struggles but also understand themselves as identified with plant temporalities: the magnolias they want to protect are old and "like Appalachians. You have to be tough to live here."[36] And the Dirt Witches, in Sydney, are advocates for the unrestricted growth of plants as a means of addressing high urban heat, low biodiversity, and the need for vegetal movement corridors.[37]

In his 2012 essay "Resist Like a Plant!," Michael Marder writes, inspired by the Occupy movement, that traditions of sedentary, nonviolent civil disobedience invoke "a politics of space" that is heavily indebted to vegetal behavior: "When environmental activists chain themselves to trees that are about to be felled, they replicate, to some extent, the mode of being of these vegetal beings:

confined to a place, bodily manifesting their bond. . . . And when protesters pitch tents in parks or on city squares, they reinvent the strange modern rootedness in the uprooted world of the metropolis, existentially signifying their discontent by merely being there."[38] These protests are, like María Soledad's, decidedly vegetal in their rootedness; they are a form of stillness with plants that takes time to "let something of them flourish in us."[39] Many such protests also recognize the gendered dimensions of the politics of movement and unmovement. It is no accident that María Soledad chants, *in, with,* and *as* the tree, "my body, my choice":[40] her refusal to move emerges from a place of feminist affinity in which both she and the tree resist being caught up in a masculine-capitalist temporality of appropriation, commodification, displacement, and development. Women have often been confined against their will and share an experience of involuntary boundedness with potted plants. At the same time, ecofeminist protests rally against enforced speed and progress made in the name of mobility, a "freedom to move" that is achieved primarily by displacing bodies, spaces, and relationships that are *in the way.*

Of course, as Infante also recognizes, plants move in their own ways, and (some) women move along with them in theirs: this sense of *shared* movement and futurity *against* masculine-capitalist progress is especially powerful in both the play and the larger politics that surrounds it. Sitting *in, with, for,* and *as* trees is not an arrest of all motion; it is, instead, a reclaiming of unmovement that aims to allow nondominant speeds and temporalities to flourish and find room to grow. Marder wonders about the importance of temporalities of decay to protest movements;[41] we also wonder about spreading, leafing, curling, blooming, branching, rooting, swaying, creeping, photosynthesizing, and respiring; about circularity, seasonality, multiplicity, and asynchronousness; about thinking and moving from a place of consciousness of being a body that is both traversed and enabled by the often-demanding temporalities of other bodies; and about welcoming the humility of being carried or of tracking the sun. Vegetality involves multiple temporalities of movement; ecofeminist and other protests and refusals may allow us to pause for long enough to recognize that even human animals can be part of this multiplicity.

Notes

1. All quotations from *Estado Vegetal* are, unless otherwise noted, as worded the script. As our essay is based on engaging with a recording of Salinas's performance, however—not on reading the script—some elements of her improvisation in this specific performance are also included and noted as such.

2. From the performance.

3. From the performance.

4. Julietta Singh, *Unthinking Mastery: Dehumanism and Decolonial Entanglements* (Durham, N.C.: Duke University Press, 2018).

5. Karen Warren, ed., *Ecofeminism: Women Culture Nature* (Bloomington: Indiana University Press, 1997); Linda Tuhiwai Smith, *Decolonising Methodologies: Research and Indigenous People* (London: Zed Books, 2012).

6. Val Plumwood, "Ecofeminism: An Overview and Discussion of Positions and Arguments," *Australasian Journal of Philosophy* 64, no. 1 (1986): 120–38.

7. Dov Koller, *The Restless Plant* (Cambridge, Mass.: Harvard University Press, 2011).

8. Luce Irigrary and Michael Marder, *Through Vegetal Being* (New York: Columbia University Press, 2016); Rosi Braidotti, "Posthuman Critical Theory," in *Critical Posthumanism and Planetary Futures,* ed. Debahsish Banerji, 13–33 (San Francisco: Springer, 2016).

9. Theophrastus, *Enquiry into Plants* (London: William Heinemann, 1916).

10. Theophrastus, 191.

11. Charles Darwin, *The Movement of Plants* (London: John Murray, 1880).

12. Darwin, 283.

13. Matthew Hall, *Plants as Persons: A Philosophical Botany* (New York: SUNY Press, 2011).

14. Darwin, *Movement of Plants,* 307.

15. Ken Thompson, *Darwin's Most Wonderful Plants* (Chicago: University of Chicago Press, 2018).

16. Monica Gagliano and Michael Marder, "What a Plant Learns: The Curious Case of *Mimosa pudica*," *Botany One,* August 13, 2019, https://www.botany.one/2019/08/what-a-plant-learns-the-curious-case-of-mimosa-pudica/.

17. Oliver Gaycken, "The Secret Life of Plants: Visualizing Vegetative Movement, 1880–1903," *Victorian Science and Visual Culture* 10, no. 1 (2012).

18. Prudence Gibson and Monica Gagliano, "The Feminist Plant: Changing Relations with the Water Lily," *Ethics and the Environment* 22, no. 2 (2017): 125–47.

19. Singh, *Unthinking Mastery.*

20. Hank Chapot, "Tree Sitting, since 1930," *Berkeley Daily Planet,* June 26, 2008, https://www.berkeleydailyplanet.com/issue/2008-06-26 /article/30396?headline=Tree-Sitting-Since-1930.

21. Shaun Barnett, "Occupy the Forest: The 40th Anniversary of a Turning Point in New Zealand Conservation," *New Zealand Geographic,* no. 153 (November–December 2018), https://www.nzgeo.com/stories/occupy-the -forest/.

22. Ari Schneider, "How Aerial Activists Are Protecting the Last of Tasmania's Old Growth," *Forbes,* September 2020, https://www.forbes.com /sites/arischneider/2020/09/08/how-aerial-activists-are-protecting-the -last-of-tasmanias-old-growth/.

23. See Michelle Gamage, "Someone Is Going to Be Seriously Injured or Killed," *The Tyee,* September 27, 2021, https://thetyee.ca/News/2021/09/27 /Someone-Going-To-Be-Injured-Killed/. Land defenders have experienced violent police racism on the blockades, meaning that it is much safer for some people to be politically immobile in these ways than it is for others.

24. Julia Butterfly Hill, *The Legacy of Luna: The Story of a Tree, a Woman, and Her Struggle to Save the Redwoods* (New York: HarperCollins, 2000).

25. Richard Powers, *The Overstory* (New York: W. W. Norton, 2018).

26. Chaone Mallory notes that, in some of these radical, more "macho" organizations, tree-sitting has also been an occasion for sexual violence against women activists. See "Ecofeminism and Forest Defense in Cascadia: Gender, Theory, and Radical Activism," *Capitalism, Nature, Socialism* 17, no. 1 (2006).

27. Vandana Shiva, *Staying Alive: Women, Ecology and Development* (London: Zed Books, 1988).

28. See Suzanne Simard, *Finding the Mother Tree: Discovering the Wisdom of the Forest* (New York: Penguin, 2021).

29. Simard also makes a thinly disguised appearance in *The Overstory* as Patricia Westerford.

30. See https://climatefactory.com.au/.

31. See https://www.pocketforests.ie/.

32. Niamh Moore, *The Changing Nature of Eco/Feminism: Telling Stories from Clayoquot Sound* (Vancouver: University of British Columbia Press, 2016).

33. Drew Philp, "America's Tree Sitters Risk Lives on the Front Line," *The Guardian,* May 26, 2018, https://www.theguardian.com/environment/2018 /may/26/tree-sitters-appalachian-oil-pipeline-virginia-west.

34. Shannon McDonagh, "Women Are Marrying Trees to Save Them from Being Cut Down," *Euronews.green,* October 14, 2021, https://www.euronews .com/green/2021/09/12/over-70-women-marry-local-trees-to-save-them -from-deforestation. For a much queerer version, see Annie Sprinkle and Beth Stephens's film *Goodbye Gauley Mountain: An Ecosexual Love Story* (2014).

35. Hill, *Legacy of Luna.*

36. Philp, "America's Tree Sitters."

37. See https://www.cityartsydney.com.au/artwork/barlow-street-forest/.

38. Michael Marder, "Resist Like a Plant! On the Vegetal Life of Political Movements," *Peace Studies Journal* 5, no. 1 (2012): 26. We underline that any politics of "occupation" needs to be complicated by a deeper structural critique of *whose* lands (and vegetal relationships) are being occupied *by whom*.

39. Marder, 31.

40. From the performance.

41. Marder, 30.

Manuela Infante and Marcela Salinas, *Estado
Vegetal,* 2019. Photograph by Efraín Carlos
Carbajal. Copyright Manuela Infante.

Feminist Structures
Polyphonic Networks
Sibila Sotomayor Van Rysseghem

This piece by Sibila Sotomayor Van Rysseghem, a member of colectivo LASTESIS and adjunct professor at Universidad de Valparaíso, is presented here first in English, then in Spanish.

Des-structures
or deconstruction?
Vertical hierarchical structures in tension,
in flames of destruction, fires of re-construction.

The search for new harvesting narratives that threaten the hero's narrative.
Collective and expansive narratives that destabilize the ascending hierarchical order.
Collective narratives that blur the issuing genius and multiply in entropic polyphonies.
Collective narratives that branch out among tuber and plastic networks.

IN THE NETWORKS WE SEE THE POTENTIA, OUR POTENTIA.
The network that emerges from the millennial fabric which branches out a common history.
A twisted rhizomatic thread composed of multiple stories, lives, and violence.
An exponential and intersectional rhizome.

It's an indeterminate and endless network, a network that unfolds, expands, and translates into new weavings without a nucleus or original model. There is no mother root but rather an a-signifying

*and cartographic rupture of new paths in constant modification. It
is an epistemological and methodological model that seeks to break
hierarchies. A model that seeks a network that engages in dialogue
and is affected by each one of its ramifications; ramifications that
share potentia. A network with no identifiable beginning or end; a
network that does not follow designated routes but perpendicularly
crosses ideas, territories, bodies.*

WE ARE THE RHIZOME.
We inhabit the subterranean, subaltern, and liminal networks.
In these nets we interweave our bodies.
Our voices historically mute, but rushing with strength and fury.

We are manifestations of liminal entities.
Subaltern subjects that for brief instants leave their subaltern
    position when raising their voice.
Raising a collective and multiple voice
to later return to the silence that configures us as subaltern
    subjects.

*The mute subject has been historically represented in the image
of the subordinate woman, because "if in the context of colonial
production the subordinate individual has no history and cannot
speak, when that subordinate individual is a woman her destiny is
even more deeply in the dark." Not being able to speak translates
into an absolute lack of spaces of enunciation. Nevertheless, when
women and dissidents [lgbtqia+ community] raise their voices from
their liminal and subaltern bodies, spaces of enunciation, spaces of
discussion, of shouts, songs, and choreographies, are opened from
the performance, disturbing, and at the same time evidencing, the
field of power; crossing the limitations for the formation of a base of
political action and generating a multiple and collective body linked
to the political in a different Other way, which is far from the hegemonic masculine ways.*

A power in struggle is evidenced.
A situated struggle,
an incarnated struggle.
With a partial and subjective view.

Epistemologies of articulation,
and not of representation.
And fuck representation,
WE WANT TO ARTICULATE OURSELVES WITH THE REAPPROPRIATION.

"Feminist objectivity simply means situated knowledge."

Incarnation of Otherness.
Of the different.
Of the incorrect.
Of the insurrectional.

Otherness that articulates itself until it is able to appear from the
    invisible corners
with the strength of the multiplicity of voices and bodies in
    political uprising.
Appearance and recognizability.
Existing beyond the human.

In that historically masculinized public space.
That battlefield.
Of resistance.
Of appearance.

*In the "sudaca periphery of our ruined democracies," the political po-
tentia that comes with the deployment of acts, performances, and all
kinds of demonstrations in the public space is generated on the basis
of our political imaginary that sees it as a battlefield, a territory of
resistance, a place of invention and meeting, a transitory vanishing
point. Hence, throughout our history, the dispute for public space
and for the construction of insurrectionary popular power continues. Today, more than ever, we corroborate that abandoning the
public space is not an option, since it constitutes a space in which
political openings are generated from the encounter between bodies,
in that space that belongs to everyone and to no one.*

Taking the space to translate into spaces of appearance and
    enunciation.
Evidencing, tensing, disturbing.
Generating a disruptive political performativity
that has the capacity to give form to something that did not
    previously exist.

To bring to reality what does not exist for reality.
To give body to nonhumanity.
To embrace the objectual and make use of its strategies.
To be a territory of extraction and exploitation.

And I insist: performances that break with the vertical organization, positioning themselves from the horizontal, from the collective and collaborative in which multiple bodies and subjectivities constitute a multiple body. A body that, from feminism, does not seek to be a counterculture, counterhegemonic, or people but rather a body; a political and collective body that, from the performative, has the capacity to give form; it has the power to shape something that did not exist previously.

Concrete political effects are generated from the ephemeral, effects which then manage to spread through multiple networks.
Through these acts of reappropriation of spatial and corporal territories
that together fight against the violence historically inscribed on our bodies.

WE RESIST.
Compositions in space.
Compositions in bodies.
Compositions in frequencies.

Channeling the choir through the Other voice,
the nonhuman voice, the posthuman polyphony.
Inhabiting echoes and reverberations from the roots
is the feminist disruption of the rhizomatic scene.

And it is probably more comfortable for critics to talk about post-humanism than feminism. To sustain their analysis in one of the threads that weave the whole mise-en-scène. But we cannot think posthumanism and plant and mineral inspiration without seeing feminist structures in their form.

Polyphonic networks of combat deployed in universal scenarios,
mobilizing feminist and collective rhizomatic potentia.

*References or the voices articulated with this ramification of ideas: Rosi Braidotti; Vir Cano and Laura Fernández Cordero; Deleuze and Guattari; Donna Haraway and Gayatri Spivak.

Estructuras Feministas: Redes Polifónicas

Reflexión en Torno a *Estado Vegetal* de Manuela Infante

Des estructuras
o deconstrucción?
Estructuras verticales jerarquizadas en tensión,
en llamas de destrucción, incendios de re-construcción.

La búsqueda de nuevas narrativas recolectoras que atentan contra
el relato del héroe.
Narrativas colectivas y expansivas que desestabilizan el orden
jerárquico ascendente.
Narrativas colectivas que borronean al genio emisor y que se
multiplican en polifonías entrópicas.
Narrativas colectivas que se ramifican entre redes de tubérculos
y plástico.

EN LAS REDES VEMOS LA POTENCIA, NUESTRA POTENCIA.
La red que surge del tejido milenario que ramifica una historia
común.
Un hilo trenzado rizomático compuesto de múltiples relatos, vidas
y violencias.
Un rizoma exponencial e interseccional.

*Es una red indeterminada e interminable, una red que se abre, ex-
pande y traduce en nuevos tejidos sin núcleo o modelo original. No
existe una raíz madre, sino más bien una "ruptura asignificante y
cartográfica" de nuevas rutas en constante modificación. Es un modelo epistemológico y metodológico que busca romper jerarquías. Un
modelo que apunta a una red que dialoga y se afecta desde cada una*

de sus ramificaciones; ramificaciones que comparten potencia. Una red sin principio ni final identificable; una red que no sigue rutas designadas sino que atraviesa perpendicularmente ideas, territorios, cuerpos.

NOSOTRAS SOMOS EL RIZOMA.
Nosotras habitamos las redes subterráneas, subalternas y
   liminales.
En estas redes entretejemos nuestros cuerpos y cuerpas.
Nuestras voces históricamente mudas, pero que se abalanzan con
   fuerza y furia.

Nosotras somos manifestaciones de entes liminales.
Sujetas subalternas que por breves instantes dejan su posición
   subalterna al alzar la voz.
Alzar una voz polifónica
para luego volver al silencio que nos configura como sujetas
   subalternas.

El sujeto mudo ha sido históricamente representado en la imagen de la mujer subalterna, pues "si en el contexto de la producción colonial el individuo subalterno no tiene historia y no puede hablar, cuando ese individuo subalterno es una mujer su destino se encuentra todavía más profundamente a oscuras." No poder hablar se traduce en una carencia absoluta de espacios de enunciación. No obstante, cuando las mujeres y disidencias alzan la voz desde sus cuerpos liminales y subalternos, se abren desde la performance espacios de enunciación, espacios de discusión, de gritos, cantos y coreografías, perturbando, y al mismo tiempo evidenciando, el campo de poder; traspasando las limitaciones para la formación de una base de acción política y generando un cuerpo múltiple y colectivo vinculado a lo político de una forma Otra, que dista de las formas masculinas hegemónicas.

Se evidencia un poder en lucha.
Una lucha situada,
una lucha encarnada.
Con mirada parcial y subjetiva.

Epistemologías de la articulación,
y no de la representación.

Y que se cague la representación,
QUEREMOS ARTICULARNOS CON LA REAPROPIACIÓN.

*"La objetividad feminista significa, sencillamente, conocimientos
situados."*

Encarnación de la Otredad.
De lo distinto.
De lo incorrecto.
De lo insurrecto.

Otredad que se articula hasta poder aparecer desde los rincones
invisibles
con la fuerza de la multiplicidad de voces y cuerpos en alzamiento
político.
Aparición y reconocibilidad.
Existir más allá de lo humano.

En ese espacio público históricamente masculinizado.
Ese campo de batalla.
De resistencia.
De aparición.

*En la "periferia sudaca de nuestras democracias en ruinas," la po-
tencia política que conlleva el despliegue de actos, performances y
todo tipo de manifestaciones en el espacio público se genera en base
a nuestro imaginario político que lo ve como un campo de batalla,
un territorio de resistencia, un lugar de invención y de encuentro, un
punto de fuga transitorio. De ahí que a lo largo de nuestra historia
continúe la disputa por el espacio público y por la construcción del
poder popular insurrecto. Hoy más que nunca, corroboramos que
el abandono del espacio público no es una opción, pues constituye
un espacio en el cual se generan aperturas de lo político a partir del
encuentro entre los cuerpos, en ese espacio que es de todas/todes/
todos y es de nadie.*

Tomarse el espacio para traducirse en espacios de aparición y
enunciación.
Evidenciando, tensionando, perturbando.
Generando una performatividad política disruptiva

que tiene la capacidad de dar forma a algo que no existía
previamente.

Traer a la realidad lo que para la realidad no existe.
Darle cuerpo a la no-humanidad.
Abrazar lo objetual y valerse de sus estrategias.
Ser territorio de extracción y explotación.

*E insisto: performances que rompen con la organización vertical,
posicionándose desde la horizontalidad, desde lo colectivo y colabo-
rativo en dónde múltiples corporalidades y subjetividades constitu-
yen un cuerpo múltiple. Un cuerpo que desde el feminismo no busca
ser contracultura, contrahegemónico, ni pueblo, sino que ante todo
cuerpo; un cuerpo político y colectivo que a partir de lo performativo
posee la capacidad de dar forma; posee la potencia de conformar
algo que no existía previamente.*

Se generan efectos concretos políticos desde lo efímero,
efectos que logran esparcirse por múltiples redes.
A través de estos actos de reapropiación de territorios espaciales y
corporales
que en conjunto luchan contra la violencia históricamente inscrita
sobre nuestros cuerpos.

RESISTIMOS.
Composiciones en el espacio.
Composiciones en los cuerpos.
Composiciones en las frecuencias.

Canalizar el coro a través de la voz Otra,
la voz no humana, la polifonía posthumana.
Habitar los ecos y reverberaciones desde las raíces
es el quiebre feminista en la escena rizomática.

*Y probablemente para los críticos resulte más confortable hablar de
posthumanismo que de feminismo. Sostener sus análisis en una de
las hebras que hila la puesta en escena en su totalidad. Pero no pode-
mos pensar el posthumanismo y la inspiración vegetal y mineral sin
ver en su forma estructuras feministas.*

Redes polifónicas de combate desplegadas en escenarios universa-
les, movilizando potencia feminista y rizomática colectiva.

*Referencias o las voces articuladas con esta ramificación de ideas: Rosi Braidotti; Vir Cano y Laura Fernández Cordero; Deleuze y Guattari; Donna Haraway y Gayatri Spivak.

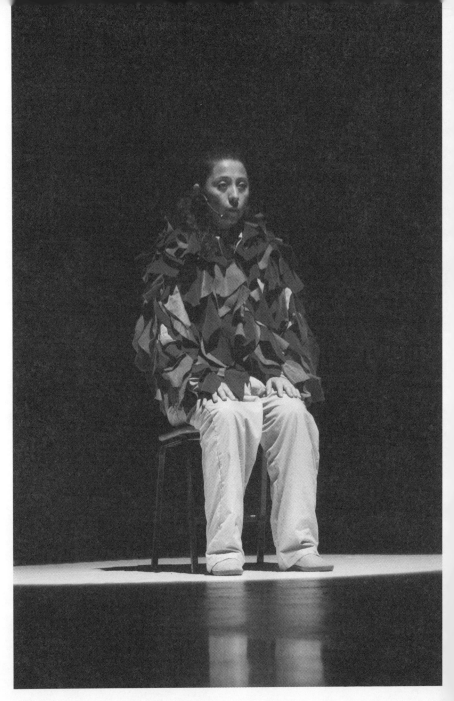

Manuela Infante and Marcela Salinas, *Estado Vegetal*, 2019. Photograph by Efraín Carlos Carbajal. Copyright Manuela Infante.

Soledad
After *Estado Vegetal*
Mandy-Suzanne Wong

> With plants we are in a constant state of loss. There's
> a separation at stake, an evolutionary separation, and
> communicative separation.
> > —Manuela Infante, interview with Giovanni Aloi,
> > *Antennae,* no. 53 (2021)

There is after all these years a part of him that feels he is wait-
ing for her. Standing on the median in the middle of the street,
he feels the sun sending out snailish feelers over the hilltops, the
roofs brown as soil with rust and green with oxidizing copper. The
leaves fuss over each other's rushing to await the light. Like this:
they like to be alike the leaves like to flush the light they shush
each other and await anticipate in flustered hush light flushing
night . . . It takes nothing at all to agitate leaves, a measly breeze, a
yawn at dawn. But without the leaves you'd never see him shiver
as he waits. Power lines dash over the streets to collide in a tangle
where the leaves meet the lightening sky; a scribble as of black
ink in which sometimes, with higher branches, he tries to read
his fortune. Sunlight sneaks into the apartment houses. They are
short and squashed together like pansies in window boxes. He
knows that when the light has slipped into the yellow apartment
house through upper windows, slanted through middle windows
in the purple apartment house beside the yellow, squatted down
and wriggled around the pale blue curtains on the lowest floor of
the shabbiest apartment house—the green one on the corner—she
will come. Unless it starts to rain. Unless her mama catches her
sneaking out before the men snoring in garbage bags have left the
median to forage in garbage dumpsters. There is no other median
in the neighborhood. This median exists only because of the tree,

the tree too big and rooted to be uprooted. Whoever colonized this land wanted no unsightly tree stumps. Therefore he lives there in solitude. In solitude she slips out of the green apartment house. María Soledad follows the soft new daylight between zipping cars and motorcycles.

She is crossing the street. María Soledad is moving. Like this: head perpendicular to rounded shoulders like a watermelon grows perpendicular to its vine. Her legs are like old branches. They have difficulty bending. Her footsteps are spasmodic shuffles of flat feet that seem unable to peel themselves off the ground. She's better at going sideways, drawing zigzags on the ground with her feet, in such fashion wriggling across the street like an earthworm. She takes an age to finish crossing, causing long cacophonies of horns, drawn-out gushes of vitriol and death wishes. María Soledad's shoulders twitch when people speak to her. The twitch becomes severe when people expect her to speak; and her words, when she can find them, sound like not words but horns. Her mama under-stands her some of the time. She tries to believe María Soledad needs no words to communicate. For María Soledad seems most content or at ease, or at least less uncomfortable, when she must neither move nor speak. Yet every yawning dawn as the leaves spread themselves before the light, she shuffles across the street to the median, to him, and says buenos días, Árbol. He's the only living tree on this split street swarming with the inert ghosts of vanquished ones hammered together into apartment houses. Each apartment house swarms with humans, and each day the humans swarm the streets with cars, buses, motorcycles, trucks, skateboards, high heels, high-end shoes made just for running. They are so unlike the leaves whose joy is unrushed hush lush love let's share the light and water with the grass. But María Soledad's solitude is like his solitude, surrounded as they are by neighbors who go too fast.

Their loneliness isn't an absence of family but has to do with multiplicity and time. María Soledad has her mama; other ten-ants of the green apartment house, several of whom, like her, have lived there all their lives; and the people who shout at her while she inches across the street. He has the light, air, clouds, grass, fungi, power lines, shoppers smoking, tramps snoring in garbage bags, the daytime drunks, all of which he is obliged to interact with somehow. He knows many languages. But he also has him-self. He lives with himself as many others. He keeps company with himself by being himself and being others at the same time, and this is what people cannot understand about him. A lot of things about him people cannot understand, but his decentralized con-sciousness is the thickest and thorniest. The idea that each branch and leaf thinks for itself, that his roots get up to all sorts of things without his branches knowing, that his bole is where he feels most like the individual he is even as he feels his plurality, and that for him to be "him" to María Soledad makes as much sense as any-thing else: people with heads cannot wrap them around these basic facts. They might if they were cephalopods. But as this isn't a neighborhood of cephalopods, the sole exception to the neigh-borhood heads' inability to wrap around Árbol might be the head of María Soledad. That head is in many respects no more than six years old. It's also the head of a woman with four decades inside her, with abaxial streaks of white and the skin around her eyes tending to rugose. It's as if time moves for her not as it moves for other humans, each moment dashing forward to crash into the next, but slowly and sort of sideways. Her moments are spiral shaped and oozy. A tree who's simultaneously ancient roots and newborn leaves can appreciate such a moment. Other people can-not wrap their heads around María Soledad. Given her so-called developmental challenges and *difficulties in communicating,* as po-lite circles describe her awkwardness, people have difficulty call-ing her a woman. If she's a woman, she's a stunted one, they think, as though her propagule were planted in too small a pot. Yet they find it just as difficult to think of her, four decades ancient, as a child. Comparisons have been drawn between her brain and over-ripe cabbages. Privately some people wish María Soledad could be reclassified phylogenetically as something else, something be-sides *Homo sapiens.* Only nobody can think of anything.

María Soledad is looking at three leaves. Two are on the grass on the median. The third is on the hip of the man who is snoring, wrapped in garbage bags and smells, at the base of Árbol's bole. María Soledad looks at the leaves with a vacuous expression, mute and slack-jawed with the expectation of drool. She has followed the sunlight trickling through Árbol's branches to those three leaves. María Soledad knows them for Árbol's leaves. And because she's the human she is, because he is the tree he is, and neither could be mistaken for anyone else, the fallen leaves seem to cry in silence to be taken up. María Soledad puts them gently in her green shirt pocket. After bending for the leaves, she must brace herself for rising with her hands against the man's broad hip. She also uses him as a step stool to the lower branches. María Soledad climbs the tree like a declawed sloth. The man who is her step stool endures her without waking; she does this every morning. When this man is in the drunk tank, Árbol offers a convenient burl. It says something to Árbol that María Soledad chooses to step on the man whenever possible instead of on his burl. The burl is like a bunion on his poor bole, which aches all the time from nails being driven into it. It says something to María Soledad that Árbol lets her climb on him even though she's a big girl now. He commits to not letting her fall, a commitment he expresses by being. His branches bear her with inborn strength. His bole, meeting the branches at certain angles, supports her in the fork where she likes to sit. His leaves shelter her from sun, his scent from smog. For forty years, María Soledad rises with the sun, nestles in the crown of her old friend, and stays until the sun retires. It is the one commitment in which she's ever succeeded.

She more often forgets things. Sitting in the tree, she says: Árbol, you dropped them. Her voice is as if sodden with sleep or drink. I brought them back, she says. She brings the fallen leaves out of her pocket. She arranges them in an axil where some of their younger siblings come together. She doesn't see, Árbol is trying to tell her: siblings curling in round their edges because wishing not to shush the sun, they hush their thirst by curling. Roots don't know about the sun but know Earth is too hot, making water hard to find when rain stays away, away rain stays when Earth is too hot. Árbol isn't thinking of this connection: leaves' hush—roots' unknowing. He's telling María Soledad: Leaves relinquish so others can survive, some leaves, hush, we must, no fuss, let go. He says it three times, each time with just one word. The leaf that falls is his word that says it all. María Soledad, knowing one way to ask questions, is laboriously formulating sounds. She doesn't understand what he's saying about sacrifices, doesn't notice the three leaves have fallen to the ground again. She's forgotten them already. With all her stiff limbs María Soledad is fluid, squeezes

out questions like sap. All her questions are old questions drip-
ping through her to decompose so she can drink them up again.
What he finds difficult is that, having asked one question, she goes
straight into the next, or so it seems. To María Soledad, her si-
lences seem ample; she can be silent for days at a time. But a day
to Árbol is a blink, even as dry afternoons are long. Her questions
seem to him to stream forth like the slime that makes snails slippery and impossible to keep up with. At the same time it seems
their discussions leave her in the dust. Hasn't he already said his
word three times? His memory isn't what it might have been;
sometimes he repeats himself. With at least fifteen senses over
and above her five, he's aware María Soledad means well. He is patient, explains again. She is patient. She inquires again. Day after
day they go on sweetly talking past each other, their intimate dis-
encounters as true and selfish as love.

María Soledad's questions go like this: *When you lose a leaf,
how do you keep from crying? When it rains, how do you keep from
sticking your tongue out? When the sun is scorching, how do you
keep from moving?* The soil of much human empathy is solipsism.
María Soledad's sense of empathy is rooted in María Soledad.
Rooting for resonance means staying rooted in herself while peek-
ing out. Plural as she is, she's too human to dare to try scattering
herself—and from wherever she ends up, looking around. She's lain
her head against his bole. Her questions are epicormic shoots of
negativity sprouting from her simple heartwood. Why isn't Árbol
more like her? Aspects of him, sensitive to subtle vibrations, realize their love was born in her solitude's alfisol. There she digs for
similarities, reverberations, more than their shared dissimilar-
ity to others. She wants to feel in every moment: his feelings and
hers committed to mutual attunement. How do you keep your legs
from twitching? she asks. There's no answer. He has no idea what
she's on about. Nonetheless, entangled in his paradoxes, María
Soledad has said to her mama: *The tree is not one, it is many, the
tree speaks with all its voices.* Her outlook is somewhat wobbly.

His perspective, too, is unsteady with the hesitant egotisms of
a gentle being that wants to live: with chemoreceptors, mecha-
noreceptors, photoreceptors, hygrometers, and inconceivable
sensoria suffusing him, Árbol's experience of life on the median
can be overwhelming as he breathes noxious miasmas from cars

and motorcycles, garbage trucks, clotheslines, kitchens, distant factories; his roots buzzing with invertebrate and mycorrhizal gossip, thunder underground from multi-axle trucks, foul flavors from industrial pollutants, the chemical stings of which he must remediate himself, through his roots, as he redresses the mildew from plastic bags discarded on the median, the corroding nails and stale adhesives binding posters to his bole, the acids in the substrate from incontinent men and boys—none of which this tree was born knowing how to deal with, none of it except insects and fungi having had any place in his ancestral forest—and every vibration is honed to a terrible sharpness by the grasping impatience of pedestrians, contempt of children spitting on the grass, fury of drivers who shout at María Soledad, vanity of ubiquitous canned music, despair of men in garbage bags, and, yes, the wounded love of María Soledad, yes, her slack-jawed anguish and unreasonable hope, all of which assails Árbol's suprasenses all at once many times over in every moment, while the prisoner in him circles round and round the empty question: Why this?

In his mind and minds, he's a tree but not a tree. Rather, he's a tree but doesn't often feel like one and doesn't know what he does feel like if not the tree he is. Buried alive beneath the asphalt longer than he can remember, his roots consider themselves commitments. They're wakeful. They are keen. Possessed of vaster knowledge than anyone imagines. Árbol's roots are the neighborhood's deep secrets. His are the nerves of this place. His roots embody his age-old promise: he has promised to be here. Part of him wonders if the place has kept its promises. Conflicting feelings on this matter churn his feelings for María Soledad into turmoil. Between the bole she embraces, the leaves to whom she unmelodiously sings, and the roots, who know best how things should be, he finds himself loving and despising her. She seems to want to be some sort of adopted leaf. But her creeping and hanging are the ways of a parasite. Árbol interrogates her like this: How do you keep from not poisoning the water? How do you keep from wilting in this noisome heat? How do you keep from witnessing the torment of our thirst? His questions are hopeless questions. He knows María Soledad didn't dig the drains. She didn't hammer the dead into apartment houses. She can't drive a car. But he has no one else. No one, no other human wonders through treehood's stillness to the hard labor of stoicism. He thinks it's because there's no purity in stillness. Stillness always hides a secret. Some secrets are silence itself. But stillness and silence aren't themselves, they hide themselves in what they're not. Because their heads cannot wrap around these things, humans disdain silence, deny anguish to the still. Only she who goes sideways when she goes at all is oblique enough to ask somebody like Árbol how not to cry. Her younger sides fear she'll never understand. Older mirrors in her know it, honor it as a reason to love him. Neither-nor aspects of her cling on, clawless and twitching. All that she is, María Soledad, is there. On the median, with him, she stays and listens to him. Other humans scorn the median as a shameful reminder: they yielded to a plant. The median is the stockade they built for condemning that lone rebel to public disdain. How do you keep from realizing you live inside the dead? How do you keep from knowing all my closest kin were massacred? How do you keep from seeing I am not what I should be? Sometimes he understands her sense of powerlessness. Sometimes he cannot understand it and wishes for a storm so he can shake himself with fury because it's all her fault! His anguish and derangement are for her sake as a descendant of conquerors. María Soledad is just María Soledad; but because she's María Soledad, she's also one of them, a human, whether they like it or not.

She's nyctinastic. She sits in the tree all day. But her mama calls her down to sleep at night, and María Soledad withdraws like an Ipomoea. Or just another spore, thinks Árbol in the dark. Subtract María Soledad, and all humans are identical parasitic spores. Árbol in the dark calls her a dissembler and betrayer. He misses her, despises missing her, despises her for missing how easy it is for him to forget reality, how cruel it is to leave him to remember all alone: reality is not at all like her. The neighborhood at night stinks, speeds, screeches marginally less than in daytime. Parts of him can't sleep and in the dark cannot distract him from himself or from the neighborhood. In those parts Árbol is always in the dark. His roots, prescient, percipient, have never touched the light, never sensed humans' emotional emanations, never known María Soledad. Roots concentrate on what trees should know. Árbol in his roots must calculate his way through the drought. Like this: plus root fine plus taproots deep plus suberin minus water loss belowground plus stress hormone abscisic acid, up signal abscisic acid, leaves plus abscisic acid minus growth minus open stomata plus lignin plus cell-wall thickness minus water loss aboveground . . . A treed human is just another thing to be survived. Down in his roots Árbol doesn't know María Soledad and therefore does not forgive her. He forgives no one underground where imbalances taste vile, the rich darkness of his loam defiled, making himself to himself taste vile. His roots remember what aboveground he's forgotten; they sing the ancestral forest. They seek it everywhere, listen for distant news of it. They smell decay and dryness coming, but they've resolved to hold fast. They're plotting with bacteria, fungi, rats, and weeds to break into the underground pipes someday. All that precious water funneled to those horrible apartment houses, those hollow golems swathed in so much fuming color they've forgotten they are trees' dismembered corpses. The roots will bide their time until the underworld is ready. Roots' time is a far cry from leaves' diurnal swinging. Árbol's roots are aware of Árbol's circadian rhythms but also of miles and miles of simultaneities. Roots' time is quantifiable according to precise assessments of chemicals, minerals, messages in near and distant soil. Times of sufficiency and dearth, times of searching and sacrifice, are but attributes of a rooting moment.

Árbol's roots can't fathom why Árbol's branches think they have time and energy to spare for María Soledad's dead weight and senseless babble. Hush hush, say tender leaves. But roots contend any human's babble must conceal an impossible, poisonous demand; and roots are experienced, focused, farsighted where fleeting leaves are flighty. All humans do is make impossible, poisonous demands, thinks Árbol in his roots in the dark. His vast multiconsciousness circles round and round this idea of impossible, poisonous demands. He knows it's not because he wishes it, but a storm comes as he wished for it that very night. A dry storm, all wind and dust, noise and lightning, it inflames his thirst and roils his septic anger. He thrashes in the wind, hissing like a mob. The power lines above are whip-wielding overseers. They catch him, they catch branches and dismember leaves, they make him scream, but he won't be undone. He is older, he is stronger: We are stronger, rush his leaves to gush, *We won't go*. All his thrashing crashing disembowels a power line, and sparks go flying. All the lights in the neighborhood go dark. An off-duty fireman who ought to be more sensible is dashing through wind and lightning on a motorcycle when sparks fly from the power line and all the lights go dark—except his motorcycle's cyclopean headlight and all the other people's headlights around the median. How does he keep from seeing the median and the large tree who's always been there? How does the neighborhood keep from hearing Árbol's howl of pain when the motorcycle crashes into his bole? Pain runs him through from highest leaf to deepest root. The screams of the great tree fill the air with pungent silence. The grass on the median and the weeds in the sidewalk brace for danger as his agony rolls on and on, down into the rhizosphere and up into the yawning dawn. All the neighborhood's ears are too animal to hear him.

Except perhaps María Soledad's. Whether the endless wail she hears is Árbol's or the sirens', María Soledad struggles bodily against her mama until everyone has gone except the yellow tape and a repair team from the power company. The tape gives way to María Soledad. The repairmen shout at her but will not touch her; they're not policemen, they're not paid to deal with lunatics. María Soledad's mama is shouting that the tree doesn't have a scratch, you idiot, it smashed that boy to a pulp. María Soledad sees only Árbol, Árbol, and she's doing so much twitching that the people on the median are revolted. Dread of misunderstanding and assault charges restrains everyone. María Soledad climbs up and sits in her fork, puts her arms around Árbol, her ear against his bole. Hush hush, she says, raining on him tears and kisses. And now she refuses to come down. Now that the tree has betrayed its community by smashing in the face of one of their fastest native sons; now it's obvious to all—the vegetation on the median requires rehabilitation via loss of limb—now the neighborhood fruitcake has treed herself and won't come down. Daylight fades out of the sky. Insistence drains from the hoarse shouting of María Soledad's mama like this: plus exhaustion plus humiliation minus hope minus will to carry on . . . María Soledad can't understand her mama's anger. She soon forgets to hear her mama, and this forgetfulness is María Soledad's commitment to the tree. María Soledad holds on to Árbol, hush hush, through the night. The storm is spent but triumphant; the winds tease the leaves in the dark. Some of Árbol's leaves smell like smoke and have gone dark forever. The power line that burned them takes no responsibility even for its own repair. María Soledad doesn't know how to acknowledge her responsibility as a dependent of power lines. She's incapable of making fire-scars. María Soledad is sitting in the tree on the median in the middle of the night, blowing gently on his branches as she'd blow on a skinned knee to soothe it. Her intense wish for the pain to end, the wounds to heal, is a quiet energy too small to glow but keen enough to feel suprasensibly almost like a gift of nutrients from a rich neighbor. Such a gift in the ancestral forest would go to the roots. But on this strange, inverted night, when the men in garbage bags have fled the median but she has stayed—María Soledad is staying through the night, even as people shout at her from their candlelit windows—the verve of her commitment goes straight to Árbol's crown. With death and danger and alien infusions of love kindling confused hysteria in the leaves, yes yes a mess but rest yes rest yes yes, he forgives her everything because she came back and stayed, because they're kindred, they're alive and therefore they are kin.

Morning is sneaking up on them. Light slips into the yellow apartment house through upper windows, slants through middle windows in the purple apartment house beside the yellow, squats down and wriggles around the pale blue curtains on the lowest floor of the shabby green apartment house on the corner. María Soledad is still in the tree. Her arms hang limp around his bole. Her cheek squashes against him. Her drool sticks to him like dew. María Soledad is asleep in Árbol's arms. Traffic and fresh shouts do not awaken her. Her body knows she's where she needs to be. She's almost succeeded in forgetting the motorcyclist. Men invade the median and try to frighten her by making chainsaws growl. María Soledad looks at them sleepily. She looks as if she has no idea what they're doing there. Something in her, the long memory of her body, believes they'll go away if she stays as she is, holding Árbol, saying nothing. Árbol hasn't slept. He's busy. In the aftermath of the short-lived fire in his crown, he's self-detoxing. He is making tannins and phenolin compounds to encourage self-resprouting. His plan is to come back stronger, grow more leaves where he's been burned than he had there before. He is compartmentalizing the wound left in his bole by the motorcycle. He's building solid walls inside himself to isolate the wound. His wound is still himself but weak and sick, prone to infection. The wound is an altered self within himself. It's an unwanted extra self, which he must treat as though it was never himself. With an oxidative burst and self-expression of defensive genes, Árbol treats his own wound like a pathogen. The motorcycle has driven him to war against himself. He besieges himself, ambushes himself; he convinces himself that the dangers from without have only just begun, and he rushes to manufacture defensive chemicals, steel himself against the future, warn the others whom he knows full well are dead.

María Soledad thinks today's clouds look like yesterday's. She is unhearing her mama, the chainsaws, people on the median shouting threats. She's as desensitive to sirens as she tries to be to shouting. In ultrasonic panic Árbol is reaching for María Soledad, he is straining to reach her. In polyphonic paranoia he unrecognizes her, he hyperrecognizes her as self, nonself, altered self. In his branches she's his champion, in his roots she is to blame, in his bole he is too busy to bother about her. She can't hear Árbol, but she tries when she remembers. She's missed hearing the rumors sporing and dispersing. Like this: if María Soledad hadn't monopolized the vegetation on the median as though it were her property, preventing it from being properly taken care of, then the authorities could've kept the tree in check; all this excessive growing wouldn't have been allowed, the thing would never have been permitted to snatch the power lines and there would've been no blackout; ergo that boy would have been spared his terrible suffering and the destruction of his motorcycle; ergo María Soledad deserves to be arrested for attempted voluntary manslaughter. María Soledad is sitting in the tree. She is singing unmelodiously to his leaves. She expresses her commitment by being. Being María Soledad means being there with Árbol, learning how to be like him: when conformity is impossible, how to survive in solitude, unmoving, unmoved. Roots know no tree needs a human to speak for them. Deep in the ground he resents her imposition. High in the sky he resents his resentment. His hard-heartedness devastates his own young leaves, where he refuses to give up on her. A policeman on the median is warning her mama that if María Soledad remains unresponsive, she will be removed from the tree by force (not for the first time, as this policeman understands it) and committed to an appropriate institution where she can do no further damage. Her lack of remorse or even sympathy for the boy and his motorcycle is described as chilling. Árbol is too frenzied to notice the policeman. As they'd order the sacrifice of parasite-infested leaves, his roots demand the branches infected with María Soledad banish themselves by abscission. The branches demand the roots acknowledge the unique nutriment that they derive from being cherished by María Soledad. Her commitment to vegetation instead of to her own community's native sons is described by her community as inhuman. Her excessive commitment to a thing, to (let's face it, says the policeman) an overgrown weed, is treason of the most disgusting sort: caring more for others than for kin amounts to inviting death into their midst. The leaves profess that they can smell her wishes, yes, her wishes all for leaves caress, wishes caressing express wishing success yes . . . The roots: scream plus speed plus scream plus speed unto ultrasound equals minus minus minus minus people who can hear minus humans. The policeman speaks for the community: A human so inhumanly committed of her own free will must be committed even against her will to someplace safely compartmentalized from the community. Árbol suspects he must at some point have suspected that humans are too fast for many things but too slow to hear screams. Rushing in his suffering he misses the din on the median. He wouldn't in the least understand it even if he listened.

Note

Italics indicate quotations from *Estado Vegetal* by Manuela Infante and Marcela Salinas.

Manuela Infante and Marcela Salinas, *Estado
Vegetal,* 2019. Photograph by Fundación
Teatro a Mil. Copyright Manuela Infante.

In Conversation
Manuela Infante and Giovanni Aloi

Giovanni Aloi: I wanted to begin by talking about plants and your personal relationship with plants. Plants in your childhood, plants in your home . . .

Manuela Infante: I grew up in Victoria, Vancouver Island [British Columbia], so in my childhood, I was surrounded by lush forests. Also the lady that works with my grandmother loves herbs and was always collecting cuttings, grafting branches to root and grow into full plants. I used to love lantana—it grew where I lived. I was fascinated by the myriad of tiny flowers composing a large umbrella—the fractal composition was interesting.

GA: Do you have houseplants, and where do they come from?

MI: I have never bought plants. They come from friends as a present or have been grafted from other plants. Others come from previous homes I lived in; they have traveled with me. The lady who takes care of them during my absence might bring me a new one once in a while. And sometimes plants just appear out of nowhere. They arrive on the terrace from the air or birds. I have an eight-foot-tall cactus on the terrace, and I have no idea where it came from.

GA: Plants have become central to contemporary conversations in science, philosophy, and art. When I started to become involved in academic discourses in the early 2000s, the main focus was on animals. And it was interesting to see how plant studies emerged from the basic nonanthropocentric notions that were developed at the time. I was impressed with Michael Marder's work and his ability to reposition plants within the discourses of Continental philosophy from which they had been excluded pretty much all along.

MI: Yes, I ran into his work pretty early on, and it really struck a chord with me. I also like his work on fire and other subjects like a few short articles he wrote on deserts. I read *Plant-Thinking, The Philosopher's Plant,* and *Graft,* and other essays. His thinking really helped me to develop my views on the subject. I wrote him an email about my project, and he was very supportive. I was very excited when he ended up agreeing to write an article in this book about *Estado Vegetal.* The whole thing comes full circle. When you are an artist engaging with academic thinking and text, one of the most exciting things that can happen is to have the authors who inspire write about your work—to me, that's an accomplishment.

I have also read the work of Stefano Mancuso and Monica Galliano, but Marder's work is by far the most influential on my work.

Both Stefano and Michael saw *Estado Vegetal* and were very interested in how their ideas have, shall I say, translated, into a different discipline. But *translation* is not really the right word. Theatre is a form of material-thinking, so it cannot be a translation but rather a dimension in which their ideas have "lived on," traveled, metamorphosed into a different state.

GA: What do you think interested them about transformative process?

MI: I see theatre as a kind of pressure chamber in which ideas can be expressed and tested. There is a certain kind of thinking that can happen within the structure of academia. But I don't think that academic institutions and structures allow for things like unknowledge, obscureness, and mystery to play important roles.

In its incorporation of sound, light, time, and text, theatre provides something like a miniature model of the world in which you can observe and explore the movements of a much bigger, ungraspable and self-organizing unit. And that's very important to me in my thinking and in my practice since my concern is with the nonhuman. A lot of what I do as a director is about letting things self-organize. That's why I like to work in the arts, because it allows me to dance around things instead of speaking about things directly.

GA: Are you an avid reader of theatre studies theory?

MI: I don't read theatre theory, and I don't read fiction either. I find it hard to get a novel in my head. I read philosophy, and I used to beat myself about my lack of interest in theatre theory and fiction. The world tells you that's what you have to read. But then I realized that philosophy and theory are fictions. They are creative perspectives onto the world and constructions of a world. I read theoretical and philosophical thinking as if they were dramatic pieces. That's how I understand it. When I read Derrida, I thought of it immediately as a play. I couldn't help myself. I would read these texts as blueprints for dramaturgical structures that could be adopted and probed.

GA: I have felt the same for many years, since my days back at Goldsmiths studying Derrida and Deleuze and Guattari for my MA. I focused on philosophy so much that I could not see why anything else deserved attention. What else on the philosophical landscape has been inspiring your creative growth?

MI: I came to the nonhuman subject while working on a piece called *Zoo*—a play commissioned by a theatre in Germany, to "celebrate" the bicentennial of Chile's independence from its European colonizers. Their intention was to have a feminine and South American perspective, obviously thinking about issues of colonialism and postcolonialism. At that time, news of the repatriation of the bones of five Kaweshkar by Chilean president Bachelet became prominent.

These remains were found in the anthropology department of the University of Zurich. They were the remains of people who had died in European countries while on "tour" as exhibition pieces in one of the human zoos that since the end of the 1800s became a tremendously popular practice in Europe; to expose "exotic" peoples from "the non-Western world." Inspired by this, I decided to take a critical stance with regard to the nature, history, and heritage embedded in the invitation itself.

I put on a piece that was quite cynical: converting the invitation that had been made to me into a kind of contemporary human zoo. We invented an ethnic group, the Tzoolkman. We crafted a language, customs, and divinities. We took a bit of the Slekman, a bit of the Yaghan, and a bit of our imagination without any discrimination between reality and fiction. And we created a mokuconference, a false paper in which two Chilean scientists presented, in a theatre in Europe, the almost completely extinct exponents of this ethnic group. Nobody knew us. I stood up in front of the public and said that instead of doing a play, I had brought with me some important Chilean scientists who were desperate for funding in Chile and needed a platform to present their research.

There was some criticism of the documentary theatre involved in the gesture. Next was an hour and a half when scientists—poor, with absurdly precarious means and methodologies—presented the Tzoolkman to the audience. Their radical problem soon surfaced: they were trying to preserve this culture. However, their main survival tool was imitation. This I took literally from Darwin's notes in the diaries of his trips to Tierra del Fuego. "They are excellent imitators: every time they saw us coughing or yawning, or making some strange movement, they immediately imitated us. They could repeat with perfect accuracy each word in a prayer addressed to them." This information became the main feature of our invented Tzoolkman peoples: when they felt threatened, they "imitated."

In a tragicomic turn, we discovered that the scientists who spoke to us were no more than the Tzoolkman already completely transformed into the scientists who had them captured. And that the real scientists acted as Tzoolkman to activate the performance of the Fuegians and prove their point in front of us. It's a work built on Darwin's notes and inspired by the text *Mimesis and Alterity* by Michael Taussig, the discoveries of neuroscience on mirror neurons, et cetera.

I then encountered Jean Luc Nancy's *Listening* and the distinction between sound and meaning. After that, I ran into Jane Bennett's *Vibrant Matter* and Bruno Latour, pretty much at the same time. His actor-network theory was very important to me and my practice at first. The reconceptualization of actors as actants, and how an actant is simply a source of action, human or nonhuman, expanded my conception of what an actress onstage could actually be. I am always looking for opportunities to mess up the theoretical framework of theatre, so that was perfect. I thought, what if I transplant these ideas into theatre: what happens? I then got into speculative realism.

From these ideas emerged the image of a person speaking to a plant. At first, I actually envisioned a person speaking to an audience of plants. The piece used to be called "A Conference to Plants." Then I found myself immersed in feminist materialism. I read Donna Haraway and the work of object-oriented feminists. That's where the idea that objects remain somewhat obscure and inaccessible to each other emerged. Now I am reading a book titled *Anthropocene Feminism* edited by Richard Grusin. I have not yet delved deep into the Anthropocene discourses, but since my next play is very likely to focus on rocks, I feel like it will be the next thing for me to explore. To take a critical stance toward the reiteration of the human as a unitary identity that the Anthropocene enacts.

GA: Why rocks?

MI: I am not an academic, so my use of all these ideas and concepts is very irresponsible and deliberately inaccurate. But from a critical perspective, a common thread among all the nonanthropocentric, new materialist, posthuman works I have read is this tendency to imprint, to reflect life onto everything. I started calling it *bionormativism*: *life* as a norm that exerts its specific forms of oppression and exploitation. Then, I found that Katherine Behar calls the same phenomenon *vivophilia.*

After months of research, I have come to believe rocks, as nonliving things, may function as models for a different kind of political resistance. They may shed critical light on the current hegemonic rhetoric of life—and the living—ingrained in concepts central to our political and economic present, such as growth, progress, development, et cetera. So the question arises: what can we learn from rocks? What could arise from the process of imitating those who have never been born, will never grow, and never die? A nonhuman, nonliving theatre? Quoting Nietzsche, "How to turn oneself to stone"?

I was profoundly attracted by how *difference* becomes radicalized when it comes to stones and rocks. Not only are they nonhuman, they are nonliving. As such, they present themselves as a territory of deep *otherness,* of implacable mystery. Prone to mystification, maybe fetishization and even capitalization.

GA: Can we go so far as to say that it is our way of experiencing life that is overimposed onto other beings?

MI: Yes, that's why Michel Marder's work stood out to me. He is not looking for us in the plant but rather for the other, for plantness, in us. The recurring panpsychism and the desire to find consciousness in everything is no longer useful to collapse the boundaries that produce the human–nonhuman distinction, not useful to think otherness as opaque, recalcitrant one could say, to use a mineral metaphor.

GA: I am interested in the point you made about anthropomorphism and panpsychism. I am also concerned with these epistemic strategies because most often they tend to reduce the otherness of nonhuman beings to mirrors into which we can see only reflections of ourselves. The underlying paradigm seems to implicitly rely on sameness: "I am interested in you because you are a bit like me." I encountered this very problem in animal studies.

It was around 2008 that I noticed how animal studies scholars marginalized insects, marine creatures, and pretty much any other animal incapable of returning the gaze. The focus was firmly kept on horses, dogs, and farm animals—all creatures we have substantially shaped and domesticated to our own benefit. That's where I started to feel that the whole approach was reductive. In my opinion, the real ontological turn was grounded in the possibility to reconceive radical otherness, not in the imposition of sameness. The question of otherness is one that encompasses the human and the nonhuman in equal measure. Transposed to the human, the question becomes, how can I recognize and value otherness into a different culture without having to spot the similarities between my culture and yours?

MI: Yes, I agree, as Mancuso proposes, I don't believe you can subject ethics to similarity.

GA: But I also understand the challenge. I believe one can only truly begin to encounter otherness when language crumbles and language cannot quite map and construct who we are and what we do. To me, that's where the work of the artistic medium begins. But that's not to say that painting, photography, and theatre don't employ language—of course, they do. I am referring to blurrings and bleedings, areas of indiscernibility and blunt contrasts.

MI: Yes, ideas of "dancing around" and "fooling around" are very important to my practice for this very reason. This very archetypical image comes to my head always, that of the origin of theatre one might say, were people dance around the fire, they can't touch it. If they did they would get burned. My previous play, titled *Realismo,* posed a conundrum. It tried out the ideas of speculative realists and also some I found in Bennett's *Vibrant Matter.* It wanted to stage assemblages and find, as she says, the perhaps small but irreducible moment of independence that things have from our perception or conceptualizations of them.

I realized that I could go about things in two ways: I could do anthropomorphic work with things or opt for documentary work instead. Either format speaks for things, or gives them a place to manifest themselves, offer a voice. I am referring more specifically to a documentaristic trend in theatre in which directors hand the stage to the subject to tell their story directly. I think this approach is very problematic in many ways. From a political standpoint, the director is still the one authorizing the performance and outlining a cultural place for it to unfold. There is a usually unacknowledged privilege involved in that kind of transaction.

With *Realismo,* I opted for the documentary route. I had these objects on stage that ultimately did not quite work in the way I had hoped. I composed this huge opera of vibrating things that turned into a tremendous source of frustration because things never did what I had planned for them to do onstage. In a way, the whole thesis was being proved, but I suffered immensely.

I somehow realized that the basic power differentials, my privilege as human trying to "make these things dance," was still untouched. That's when my strategy changed as I embarked on *Estado Vegetal.* Instead of trying to speak for plants or trying to speak about plants or even translate plants into other media, I decided to embed the idea of *plantness* throughout the structure of the work instead of representing plants. If I wanted to investigate plants and the vegetal realm, but I knew it was wrong to think I could say anything about plants, much less "represent" plants, I was not so naive as to think I could speak for them. All I could do was to speculate, imitate them, looking deeper for the plant other in me than for what of me is in them. So the task was to make a vegetal play instead of an animal play. I set out to imitate plants with the whole body of the piece itself.

I learned how to work with light, how to structure the rhythm, dramatic structure, and sound in ways that might let the otherness of plants transform theatre. I believe representation to be as problematic a concept in theatre as it is in politics. I turned to imitation as a preferred concept. Imitation as a way of physical speculation, where you try to be the other with your body.

Speculation, according to Ian Bogost, is the practice common to all things and beings, with which we try to come to terms with otherness in the world, with difference. We all speculate about what is other. To me, theatre-making, in its mimetic function, is a speculative practice. Mimesis is the practice of wanting to be other with one's body, not to know, use, interpret, or represent the other. Mimesis not as the science of knowing but as the science of physically speculating with others is a productive way of acknowledging otherness, instead of representing. This makes me think of Ian Bogost's idea that speculation is the creative practice of figuring out how the other feels itself. And that's what I like about the ambiguity inscribed in the term *speculation*. It enables a possibility to emerge, but it does not delimit or preempt the capacity of that possibility.

GA: I also think that one of the most important aspects of the ontological turn in the arts and philosophy is its ability to enrich the world. From new materialism to object-oriented ontology, nothing is static and inert, everything is agentially charged. The rejection of pacification and objectification the ontological turn advocates is also essentially important to our reconsideration of plants in contemporary culture.

Over the last century, popular culture has developed two main approaches to plants. On one hand, the majority thinks of them as objects, nonsentient architectural structures capable of growing as one's own hair does. On the other is a ridiculed minority that conceives plants as sentient beings and understands plants as akin to animals. In my opinion, the philosophies of the ontological turn insert themselves between these two polarities as a speculative interface. But in my experience, plant sentience still scares people. It certainly disturbs the implicit normativity that underscores vegan philosophies. I have been attacked more than once at conferences simply for entertaining the idea that plant sentience might exist, as science tells us. This is what troubles me. While speculative philosophies attempt to enrich the world around us, many scholars and much of the general public seem to be much happier with a reductive approach instead—they are happy to empty the world. I wonder why that would be the case?

MI: Stefano Mancuso has a humorous answer to that. He says that we behave like teenagers toward parents as we relate to plants. We are so aware that our lives depend on them that we rebel to emancipate ourselves. I think that's interesting, because it casts our reaction to plants as an automatic reactionary response, rather than a thought-through one.

GA: That's interesting, because most of the negative responses about plant sentience come from intelligent and educated individuals, and yet they cannot quite elaborate their thesis beyond dismissal and denial. They just seem to shut down.

MI: Well, what I'm about to say might sound obvious, but I think that our fear of plant sentience is also grounded in the fear of losing our privilege over the nonhuman. What I particularly like about the idea of plant-thinking, for instance, is plants' ability to change the shape of our thinking. Or Latour's idea that action does not have to be intentional changes the very notion of passivity in plants—that's enriching. The ability of many new materialist, posthumanist, more-than-human authors to recognize the diverse range of agencies surrounding us is also extremely enriching. The ability to acknowledge agencies that are not akin to human agency but that nonetheless have an impact on everything else. At the core of it all lies the impetuous to shatter a sense of fictitious unity—this constitutes an important challenge for theatre and also for everything we do . . .

GA: Yes, the need to be coherent, cohesive—which also brings us to the question of duration in theatre and how these philosophies might impact the very essence of classical theatre and performance.

How do plants impact the structural aspects of a performance? But I think that this question becomes even more important if we consider that all artistic manifestations unfold within a cultural paradigm that supposes a dialogue or an engagement factor. In other words, we don't want to creatively lose our audience so much that nobody is listening anymore.

MI: This makes me think of a question I was asked at a Q&A following a performance of *Estado Vegetal*. I was asked, "Why don't you stage this performance outdoors surrounded by plants, where you could be more on their terms?" My answer is that theatre in itself, as a cultural site, represents the constrictions of our thinking. So, I like the constraints, and I like to work within them to see how plants can inform a radical change in the way we have been thinking—and thus making theatre—up to now.

GA: Yes, I can see your point. And taking the performance outside does not automatically solve all the problems and contradictions. This brings to mind the conundrums land art faced during the 1960s and 1970s. Making art outside the gallery space didn't exactly equate to the freedom artists longed for.

MI: And that's where speculation becomes a fairer and less totalizing approach to the nonhuman. It's a somewhat more honest and also more humble approach. I am curious to see how this will apply to my next project on rocks.

GA: That's also interesting—am I right to assume that this constitutes a more radical shift in your inquiry? I am thinking more specifically about the connection between the tree at the center of your play and the resistance it poses. In that sense, your tree in *Estado Vegetal* already is a bit of a rock. It has a Heideggerian quality according to which it becomes visible to the people around it only when it stops functioning as a tree, when it burns because of the incident and when it causes an accident.

MI: Yes, I see the analogy. And the accident in the show was an accident. I never start with the narrative. The methodological path I followed entailed writing down concepts from the authors we have discussed, and I began to improvise with Marcella for hours and hours. It was like a game. Stories began to emerge, and we would allow the actants in each story to exercise their agency over the narrative. That's how these characters appeared and how they took control of the narrative. I did not follow a traditional work-flow in which one plans an accident to then pursue a resolution.

We started with an idea of branching in storytelling and modularity. We focused on how the same modular blocks can mean more than one thing in different stories. Our text was modular, just like plants, in that all narrative branches spoke with the same sentences but were completely different anyhow. Also the modularity was applied to the idea of there not being a central conceptual government, so to say, in the piece. Just like plants have all their organs repeated in all their body, and are not governed by some central brain, we learned to make a piece with no center, no unity, and this in the end is basically with no internal hierarchies. And that's a rough one to counter even in the most postdramatic of theatres.

We applied ramification to the dramaturgical structure of the piece. There is a trunk event, but we come to the story by means of branches. When a branch branches off into another branch, there is a new voice, a new character, a new perspective. The event we tell is simple: a fire fighter is coming back from putting out a forest fire, and he runs his motorcycle into a tree, ending up in a vegetative state. But this is never told like this in a linear manner, but rather in the form of a *ramified dramaturgy*. This was developed over hours and hours of improvisation, where we would practice telling stories by means of branching out all the time. Here characters and narratives emerged as a result of the formal experimentation.

GA: I found the narrative structure of *Estado Vegetal* to enhance a poetic quality and to lend itself to a certain poignancy grounded in realism. Some moments are very intensely emotional; the affective charge is tremendous. The ways in which the different voices intertwine produce a complex tapestry of emotions and affects that seems masterfully orchestrated.

MI: *Estado Vegetal* is as a composition of affects. I like this notion we have just crafted here. The performance is not a composition of texts, and it is not a composition of images. It is a composition of affects. I organize affects along a trajectory of sorts to trace an affective journey. But the journey is far from linear.

GA: It seems to me that *Estado Vegetal* capitalizes on a deliberate ambiguity, a blurring at the edges in which one character seamlessly flows into another or in which one body ventriloquizes multiple voices that never announce themselves. The mother, the girl, the old lady, the tree—the embodiment and the fluidity point toward a collective, shared state of mind, a plantlike communicative network. The viewer find themselves actively engaged in negotiating these presences in a nonhierarchical way. As the performance unfolded, I realized that clearly pitching each line to the appropriate character didn't really matter. That gave way to a beautiful overlay between human and plant akin to how I imagine trees and other plants communicate with each other through their roots and fungal networks. The result is a beautiful carpet of affect, woven in a surprisingly seamless way, producing a whole that's impossible to disentangle. It seems to me that the supporting mesh underneath the carpet is made of an idiosyncratic desire, a sense of longing that bears deep existential undertones. Quite a few moments in the performance are marked by a sense of absurdity that we are only allowed to wallow into in our private spheres. Some of the narrative threads can exist only as moments of vulnerability and intimacy in the solitary encounter between human and plant, in which one being meets another.

MI: The private sphere has been very important to me. The narratives are meant to represent our attachment to plants and consequent vulnerability to them. I think improvisation is the key here. The narratives and characters emerge as part of a stream of consciousness. They are emerging from our shared experiences of plants and the branching process.

We wanted the narrative to feel like a spontaneous process of branching out where new branching happened unannounced and new perspectives intertwined. This is part of an important question of multiplicities that I am to address through the body of one actor. We carefully considered the idea that plants are multitudes and how that might work within the context of a monologue. So the solution was polyvocality.

Mancuso talks about how plants communicate in polyphonic ways. So, at that point, we also began to think about technology and thus incorporated the looper, which Marcella uses live on stage to shatter the identity-based assumption that in theatre assigns one character to one actor. In my next work on rocks, I will be working with three actors. In the case of *Estado Vegetal,* part of the sense of intimacy that emerges from the play comes from Marcela's own loneliness onstage. But I feel there is something interesting in this postidentity and this form of understanding acting as a multiplicity construct that can be explored further. As Virginia Woolf said, "Multiplicity is the possibility to keep becoming."

GA: I wanted to ask you about the minimalism that *Estado Vegetal* seems to embody. I was fascinated by the idea that the monologue is such a classic genre in theatre, it is one of the quintessential pillars of the art forms, it is like the nude in classical painting. But I was surprised by the humorous entrance of Marcela onstage and how you slowly upturn the conventions and expectations of the monologue to great effect. I was fascinated by the absence of a tree as a visual image in the matrix of the performance and how the different narratives, in turn, contributed fragments to the image of a tree existing only in the minds of the audience.

MI: Yes, I think we approach the tree from a cubist perspective. We never described it, but we kept shedding light on it from different angles and different perspectives. The result is a tree made of situated speculations, and also a tree that remains obscure, a face of it always hidden to us.

GA: With this level of cubist fragmentation also comes a sense of loss. Trauma and loss enable the audience to effectively consider what's usually invisible in plant life, their communicative abilities and different timescales. But at the same time, it is trauma and loss that congeal a series of considerations about human life too.

MI: Trauma is a broken moment. It is when time warps. Yes, I can see how trauma and loss can induce a state that can help us to consider different timescales and perceptions. There is something about the incommensurability of trauma; it is so immense and impossible to grasp. During our improvisations, I asked Marcela to imagine the point of view of a mother coming to terms with a traumatic event. I don't think of *Estado Vegetal* as the grieving of a mother, but it was an effective tool to guide Marcela through the performance.

Ultimately, trauma is the moment of change, and that's the important part of trauma that I wanted to channel. Trauma allows access into a different dimension, and in this case, I hope that it also represents an opportunity to rip apart anthropocentrism. And in this context, loss works well, too, because when engaging with plants, we are in a constant state of loss. There's a separation at stake, an evolutionary separation, and communicative separation. Mediating loss was actually one of the most complicated aspects of *Estado Vegetal*. Sometimes Marcela would get too absorbed in the motherly loss, and I would try to bring her back to a less dramatic place because of a fear that we might involuntarily cast an image of "mother nature"—that has been quite terrifying, and I am glad to see that audiences don't seem to read the work in that way.

GA: Yes, I agree. I think it's a terrible cliché, and it would be very reductive of what you have accomplished with the performance. It seems to me that in *Estado Vegetal,* trauma reveals that a lot of our suffering is actually caused by our anthropocentric frame of mind. Through a thorough consideration of plant-being, the performance critiques the importance we attribute to notions of identity and our desire to project into the future rather than being in the moment. I read the performance as deeply existential in essence. Especially toward the end of the performance, when the red lighting accentuates a dramatic peak in the narrative—by that stage, I felt like the play had taken me through a lot already. That moment is extremely charged and meaningful in the sense that it gets away with asking important nonanthropocentric questions that would sound ridiculous if asked in a different context. It feels as if *Estado Vegetal* destroys your certainties bit by bit to then blow all the pieces away so that nothing can really be rebuilt properly.

This approach made me think of Deleuze and Guattari's becoming-animal and how different your approach is from that. As you might remember, their becoming-animal gained substantial traction during the last decade. Many contemporary artists engaged with this idea, often too literally. But there was palpable excitement about this flight—the opportunity to leave our anthropocentrism behind, at least momentarily and most regularly, performatively. The results were mixed, and eventually, the focus shifted onto animal rights and veganism, which completely changed the philosophical essence of animal studies.

To me, in that moment, it became possible to see how philosophical theory can be too easily appropriated in ways that do not necessarily generate productive thinking or good scholarship. After reading Deleuze and Guattari's *A Thousand Plateaus* while studying for my master's at Goldsmiths, I focused on Foucault for my PhD and became interested in his notion of the *event* as a transformative experience, which seems closer to what you do. It seems to me that your approach to the nonhuman and to performance is not concerned with a notion of becoming-plant?

MI: I don't believe in the notion of becoming as something possible to produce or reproduce. The notion of imitating or mimicry that Deleuze and Guattari devalue in their becoming-animal is actually important to what plant philosophy entails. The idea of developing plantlike structures is important and essential to the production of something that is not a flight from reality but that enables us to test the boundaries of reality. The becoming, or the event, happens in the audience, not on the stage; it is not within my control.

GA: Toward the end of *Estado Vegetal,* the notion of fixity becomes central. Previously in the performance, plants rebelled against the imposition of pots as a form of tyranny. Pots allow us to move plants where we think they should be, and in that sense, they infringe on their prerogative to be permanently situated somewhere—which is their nature. Later on, this point is further expanded through the consideration that plants commit to a situated life, confined to a never-ending present they have to embrace and successfully navigate—while we animals flee. If the situation becomes adverse, we abandon our surroundings and find shelter elsewhere. This powerful consideration repositions the evolutional hierarchy we have treasured since Darwin. Instead of being at the top, we are cast as evolutional cowards.

MI: Yes, there were quite a few ideas echoing this in what you have called the "red scene," the more lyrical moment. Animals "evade," when plants "face," danger. New materialist and posthuman feminism has said a lot about situatedness and location. The humanist fleeing into an "objective view" of the world, instead of having the guts to produce situated knowledge, is without a doubt a form of cowardice. I cared that we committed to the behavioral reality of plants, at least as we see it. And I think that commitment made things happen. For instance, Marcela is stuck in the center of the stage, which is something that the tradition of theatre tries to avoid. In theatre, you want to create a sense of dimensionality and fluidity and use space in dynamic ways. Commitment to a territory is multiplied in different spheres of the performance. It governs the lighting, the sound design, the writing. There's also a multiplicity of existences for these notions.

GA: Yes, and light plays an important role in *Estado Vegetal* too. I assume that much of the improvisation with Marcela you mentioned earlier must have emerged onstage directly?

MI: Yes, we considered the lighting as a key to photosynthesis, so at one point, we began to practice the notion of *phototropos*. In theatre, the light follows humans—that's the norm. We decided to reverse that and let light move the actress. These plantlike adjustments can transform your practice bit by bit. But it took a lot of practice and work.

GA: I also assume that as an actor, embracing these new ideas must be challenging.

MI: Yes, it becomes a chain of events in which a small change leads to another. Following light onstage leads to the emergence of a different type of dialogue. So, these elements start to affect each other in ways that are not controllable; this is the essence of experimentation that makes theatre like a pressure chamber. I always thought that theatre is the thing that happens in between actress and light, in between sound and words. Not in any of those things alone. So, I compose in between these things. Working from the stage becomes extremely important. In-betweenness is central to theatre, and that's what can derail the compartmentalization of ideas and concepts.

GA: Yes, that's where philosophy and other disciplines like art history, perhaps, fail to capture the in-betweenness of their objects of study. The ontological turn in philosophy has precisely attempted to accomplish that. The constrictions that humanism has placed on our understanding of the nonhuman can be easily revealed by scrutiny of our relationship with plants and the unexplored in-betweenness in which important links between us and plants lie. Art can unhinge disciplinary constrictions and limitations.

MI: Despite its conservativism, theatre can unhinge disciplinary boundaries and allow a possibility to think through a new fluidity. Putting things onstage to see what happens allows the exploration of that in-betweenness. As I said earlier, the stage is a great place to see matter self-organize. As a director, I am actually a kind of spectator of that myself.

GA: Despite the darkness, *Estado Vegetal* is also humorous. The performance begins in what seems a lighthearted tone. However, the mood changes rapidly . . .

MI: I always incorporate humor into my pieces. I have used the expression "fooling around" before, and I think that's an important methodological tool in what I do. There's something silly and lighthearted about that, an experimental openness; when fooling around, I trust where humor might take me. I can follow laughter because I trust humor as an indicator of a shift, or a change. Humor is a good star to follow when working with nonhuman topics since one cannot address them directly, so there's nothing left than learning to very seriously dance or fool around them. Marcela is a comedian. We went to school together. I have known her for twenty years. We have not worked together for a long while, but I have followed her professional development. Whatever she does is full of humor. So I have not planned the humor that dots *Estado Vegetal,* but it has emerged spontaneously in places, and I have harnessed it as a steering wheel to drive the narrative.

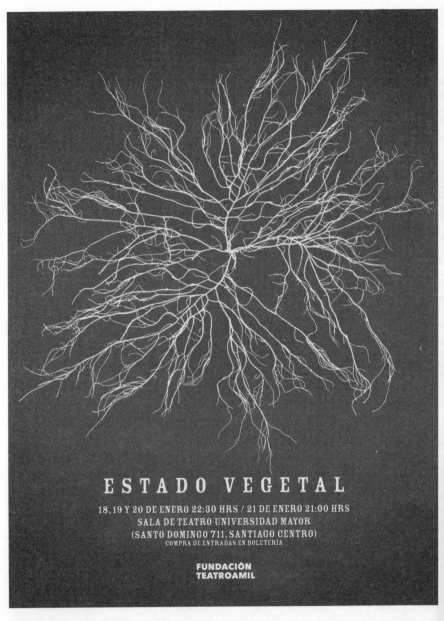

ESTADO VEGETAL

18, 19 Y 20 DE ENERO 22:30 HRS / 21 DE ENERO 21:00 HRS
SALA DE TEATRO UNIVERSIDAD MAYOR
(SANTO DOMINGO 711, SANTIAGO CENTRO)
COMPRA DE ENTRADAS EN BOLETERÍA

FUNDACIÓN
TEATROAMIL

Program cover, Manuela Infante and Marcela
Salinas, *Estado Vegetal,* designed by Javier
Pañella, 2017.

Estado Vegetal

Manuela Infante

Estado Vegetal has been performed by Marcela Salinas on stages around the world since its debut in 2016; this script of *Estado Vegetal* has been translated from the original Spanish (translation: British Council Chile, Bruce Gibbons Fell, Alex Ripp).

> Direction: Manuela Infante
> Dramaturgy: Manuela Infante, Marcela Salinas
> Design: Rocío Hernández
> Design and Props Construction: Ignacio Pizarro
> Stagehand: Magdalena Mejía
> Sound Design: Manuela Infante
> Production: Carmina Infante, in coproduction with
> Fundación Teatro a Mil

Raúl

Yes. What? Yes. Where? Here? No, I don't have a problem with being recorded, go ahead. Yes, but before I answer your question, I want to say thanks for the opportunity given to me on this occasion, for it allows me to be able . . . let's say, to clarify the proper responsibility such as it concerns me, OR DOES NOT concern me according to the facts.

We had already received several complaints on the matter of the tree when it took place . . . the event of unfortunate consequences of which we have all had news.

As a matter of fact, this lady from the neighborhood committee, no, women's center, community center which is not the same but is similar . . . Hmm, what was the lady's name? . . . At this moment, I remember her name, let's say, slightly, not to say barely. Look, it escapes me now, but once it comes back to me I will let you know. She always complained to me about the matter of the tree, because I am the person in charge of green spaces for this emblematic and beautiful borough, of which I am a native . . . yes, on my mother's and grandmother's side . . .

Let's see, so, where do I want to go with this? Because, of course, you are going to say, Don Raúl, you are beating around the bush, but it turns out that we are talking about the, how can I say this, UNRESTRAINED growth of this tree, "a growth that does not restrain itself" . . . do you understand me? Because a tree does not restrain itself; they follow the light without stopping and in every direction and at the same time! Just like say, all major cities do, as to establish some sort of paragon for your better understanding. They are . . . how to put it . . . EXCESSIVE.

Now, the fact that the branch was bound to touch the electrical cabling, we can clearly say that "we could have seen this coming." I know, you don't have to tell me. Of course, the branch was going straight to the power line . . . a line that is . . . why not say it?— LYING there. Just like, if you'll allow me, the young rider, victim of the event, was LYING there on the asphalt.

Of course, we could say that it was a just matter of looking up and one would have been able to see it coming, but the thing is, you don't see a tree move. Because what happens? A tree moves so slowly that it seems still. A tree lives for . . . how long? Hundreds of years! So then, of course, imagine your life, your very own life, stretched out to hundreds of years SLOW.

So then, of course . . . you could say "you should have seen it coming, Don Raúl," "the storm was approaching, Don Raúl," but I would have to answer: "Yes, officer, but YOU COULD NOT SEE IT." That's the central issue in all of this: this is a COMING that CANNOT BE SEEN.

So, what am I trying to get at with all this? Because, of course, you're going to say, Don Raúl, you're beating around the bush, but it turns out that. Sure,

listen, the tree was there before the streetlights were installed. I'd even dare to say that all the people currently living here in the borough came . . . let's say, after the tree. You need to get that in order to understand it. God first made the plants, the forests, the seaweed, and then he divided the seas and made the light, and then he created man in, like "the cherry on top," and later, from that man he extracted the woman. Like "the cherry on top of the cherry" if you want to comprehend it in a more contemporary, more modern, feminist fashion. And the woman ate the fruit from the forbidden tree of the Garden of Eden. She barely ate from it, not to say very little, but eat she did, and as soon as she ate they felt such great shame that . . . what did they do? . . . they covered them- selves with a LEAF. The cherries covered themselves with the cake.

Eva! . . . Eva is the name of the lady from the neighborhood com- mittee, no, women's center, community center, which is not the same but is similar. A participative lady but, God, is she insistent. Do you know that saying, "the stormy neighbor"? When people want to fool around and say inversely that "there's a neighboring storm," well this is not inversely anything, because this neighbor is really . . . boy, is she stormy! She created such a big storm that they finally gave us the green light, not the traffic light, but for the project itself. And what does the borough have to do? Just cut the tree. Carry out what is known as a "severe pruning," which means leaving it, as one would say, amputated, so as to estab- lish some sort of paragon for your better understanding. But we could never carry out the municipal operation because it always turned out the girl was on the tree; because there is a girl that lives in the house right on the corner, next to the tree. She had to be brought down from the tree on several occasions. And she cried and kicked because she has some kind of "intellectual deficiency," or "different ability" if one wants to put it in a more contemporary, more modern fashion; so it becomes quite difficult to talk to her. Initially, I would ask her: "María Soledad"—María Soledad is the girl's name—"do you realize that your shenanigans are hindering the municipal operation?" To which she answered . . . if you allow me and with all due respect: "Yes."

Hard to get to safe harbor in terms of communication. Without going any further, the very night of the event of unfortunate consequences, of which, by the way, she became a key witness, I personally tried to establish some sort of dialogue again, I asked her several questions directly:

—Did you see anything?
—Yes?
—How?
—But, who?

Girl

Did you see anything?

Yes.

Yes?

Yes. He had fallen asleep.

What?

Yes. Sleeping. Yes! He was sleeping.

But, who?

Not the motorcyclist. The tree.

Did you see anything?

He was sleeping.

Yes?

Yes, the tree had fallen asleep.

How?

Trees sleep.

But, who?

I don't know about the motorcyclist. But the tree was asleep.

Did you see anything?

Yes, in the ceiling. Black leaves.

Yes?

No, not green. Black. They moved.

How?

Like this.

But, who?

The wind.

Did you see anything?

The tree screamed.

Yes?

Yes. He speaks. He screams.

How?

Like a stadium. Like this. Haaaaa, haaaa.

The tree is not one, it is many. The tree speaks with all its voices, like an audience, like a stadium, like this:

"Haaa, haaa!"

"One more song" "One more song"

"Oh, no, we won't go" "Oh, no, we won't go"

"He who doesn't jump is a faggot, he who doesn't jump is a mummy, he who doesn't jump is a mummy, he who doesn't jump is a mummy!"

Where are your legs?

I can't move. I can't move. I can't move.

Eva

"I-ee can't mooove!!!" screamed and screamed that girl perched on top of the tree while the firemen tried to bring her down. What is that girl saying?!

"Icantmooove!!!" With that strange face she has. Of course, she is far from being a child, she is a grown woman! How old is she? About forty?! Much older than me! And I was trying to concentrate, to explain to the police, because I was the first to arrive. So I said: Look, officer, I was perfectly still, lying on my bed around 3:15 in the morning—I have problems falling asleep—when suddenly the power was cut off. And I was shocked!

Then, before I'm able to put on my slippers: boom! Because it sounded just like a bomb. It tormented me! It made me jump.

So then I leave my room and begin to knock on the door next to mine: "Carlos, please! Carlos, please!"—Carlos is my ex-husband, but we still live together—"Carlos, please!" And he stays there looking at me and goes: "Please you!" He doesn't understand a thing! So I just went out. I open the door, go out to the street, and it was all black, but I sensed a smell—it just happens that I have very delicate nostrils—and I began to follow the smell.

When I turn around the avenue corner, I open my field of vision and start seeing pieces, chunks, parts of the motorbike. And then I open my field of vision again, and a few meters away, I can see the guy's body lying in the middle of the street. "My God! My God!" I was talking to myself. Crying out.

When I got close to him, I realized: "Hey, there is nothing but broken pieces here!" "Where are your legs?" And the guy barely mumbled: "I can't move, I can't move."

Look, someone once told me: "Eva, if you ever see someone who has suffered an accident, you have to pay attention to the shoes, if the victim has both shoes on, it's because he is alive, if both shoes flew off, it's because the guy went on to the other side," but this kid still had one shoe on, so I thought: He's fighting! He's fighting for his life!

I'm thinking about this when I open my field of vision again and I see, a few meters away, the tree. It was also wounded. Geez! The leaves weren't green, they were black! Of course! The tree's branches finally touched the wires on the power line, a spark was ignited, and since it was windy the tree burst into flames—that image seems so biblical to me—and then it hit me! Of course! This kid was on his bike, the lights went out, and bam! He crashed into the tree. Then I realized that this kid was Manuel. Of course I know him because this kid lives near here, he lives with his mom, a really good lady, like super nice, like really quiet, like just really ordinary people!

He bought that bike not long ago, he pimped it and everything. He'd ride with his girlfriend. He went fast with that bike. I say, hey, "No mother ever wants their child to buy a motorcycle." Look, have you heard that saying "first have a plant, then an animal, and then a child"? I have no problem with plants, I've got my plants, my hibiscus. I love plants! I have no problem with animals, I've got my two cats and my two dogs, but when it comes to children! No! . . . It's one of the reasons Carlos, my EX, and I started to drift apart.

OK, but the issue is the tree. Let me say, that tree was an ongoing subject, I'm telling you, that just, every day . . . I mean . . . ahhhh! I complained! I complained until I got tired! I swear! With Don Raúl, this person who is "in charge of the green spaces," supposedly. I'm telling you, I have waged an all-out war with him. He should have seen this coming!

This tree was a problem, it's a giant tree. The branches had grown monstrously. But I swear it was a giant trunk, it was eating up the pedestrians' space. Stinking of pee! Because I swear, it was a public bathroom. Every time I went by, I'd see the ass of some fool who was peeing. Because, oh my God, men! Men can have a lamppost, a wall, their own bathroom too, but they choose the tree. Hey! *Homo sapiens*! You're not in the jungle! A stench that, I swear to you, fatal.

It was also a bulletin board, so tacky! It was all lined with ads. "I need this thing," "I sell this other thing," "the music teacher this," photos of lost dogs, of cats. I'm telling you, I am an animal lover, but hey . . . if you've lost an animal, you've lost it, and that's it! It wanted to leave, I don't know . . . it was run over, done!

Audio: I say, let's cut that tree. I tell you right here, that if this kid Manuel happens to pass over to the other side—may God forbid—right there, they'll place the shrine! They'll paint the tree white, glue plastic flowers onto it and, boy, any day the tree is going to just walk away on its own.

So, I say, regarding the matter of the tree, Don Raúl, do your job, please take charge of the green spaces. Remove that tree from there, apply an electric saw.

I mean the matter of the tree is one thing. But it's not just that, there's the ghost house, as they call it, a property that has been in a deplorable state for more than twenty years. You're going to say, OK, but, what has Don Raúl to do with this? Well, he's in charge of green spaces, right? And this house, I swear, I give you my word, was, it just was . . . it was . . . a jungle! The plants had swallowed it. I'm telling you, it's . . . it's just . . . That's how I imagine things when human beings are long gone from the face of the earth . . . No, I don't imagine it, I saw it on TV, when human beings are no longer on the face of the earth, it will take plants only three months to cover everything. The planet is going to be just like a big green ball.

PAUSE.

By the way, the firemen arrived. But the fire department had to take care of the girl perched on the tree, screaming, I swear, like a hog, like a pig being killed with a blunt ax.

They asked me if I was a relative since I was one of the first ones there. "No! I'm a neighbor, I don't have children." It just happens that I'm very attentive, not a leaf falls here without me knowing. And then I realized, hey, but of course! This kid has a mom, and his mom is not here! I said: "You know, officer, I don't know why I have the feeling this kid's mom hasn't heard and might be still sleeping like a log." So, I went over!

I arrive at her house; I ring the bell. Then the lady comes out.

I tell her . . . I tell her. And she tells me . . . she tells me. And I tell her . . . I tell her. And she says, "The police station," she says. So, I went over there.

I arrive at the police station, I swear I'm just arriving to the police station, when who do I run into? DON RAÚL. I could not utter a word, the only thing I said was: "Don Raúl . . . the tree." His eyes filled with tears. I let him go, I said: "Let go, Eva. This matter is not yours." I go into the police station, all is quiet, barely any movement. Suddenly Major Soto comes out—a pretty hunky guy—he comes out of his office and then I saw that the mother was there! She was inside the office, sitting down, in what I imagine to be a sort of interrogation room. And hey, it really caught my attention because I saw her, I saw her so undaunted, so immovable, just like . . . planted there. I don't have any children, you see, so I can't tell you what it feels like when one is about to lose a child, but I would imagine that one would at least cry! Right? I don't know! You despair! But not her, she was there, there so . . . so . . .

Mother

No.

Yes.

But I don't see him much because of his studies and because of his girlfriend and because of work. Because of all those things no I don't...

What?

He told me: "The bike is because of time Mum," "because I don't have time, Mum," he was always running against time, Manuel. Until he ran into a tree.

No mother ever wants *her* child to buy a motorcycle.

No, I don't want the bike, why would I...

They gave me a mirror that the police picked up. The one you use to look backward. Why would I want to look back?

He was happy with the bike. He "pimped" it. He said he had "pimped" it. Manuel always loved speed, he *could never* stay still anywhere.

Since he was young, I felt that he had too much energy, that he needed to move. So, I enrolled him in several workshops offered by the borough.

He was in basketball, swimming, karate, cooking, he even participated in a theatre workshop.

Once he was very worried because they had given him a character that couldn't move. Imagine that.

He must have been about six or seven years old.

He cried: "I can't play this, Mum, I can't move. I can't move!"

We rehearsed together. Because it was hard for him. We *even* made his costume together.

At first, he moved a lot, I remember I'd say "stay *still,* Manuel." "But the wind is blowing! There's a lot of wind, Mum!"

All the other children played people and entered and exited the stage. They had TREE lines. Some even sang. And Manuel was there, standing still, dressed as . . . a TREE.

Sees plant.

Sorry. You were asking me . . . yes, even this thing about being a fireman was because of this issue of speed. He loved speed. I have already told you Manuel is a firefighter, right? . . . Well, of course, because of all that coming and going, he would forget things. Every day his wallet, the keys, the alarm clock, every day I'd end up waking him, I had to shake him because he slept like a LOG . . .

Plant.

No, Manuel is a good kid. The thing with speed is an issue for all kids nowadays. They have this thing for always wanting to be somewhere else. It's more of a root problem.

What? No. I'm sorry; I have to go outside for a moment.

Plant. She brings plants from outside.

Mother choreography with plants.

Nora

You're very pale, you need more light, my sweetie, I'm going to put you here. Do you feel better there, hon? Great. And you, my dear, are too big, I'm going to have to do something about you, you're drinking too much water. Hey! Look at you. You keep getting blonder. You're in your prime, love. You know, I'm going to have to move you to another pot. This flowerpot doesn't suit you anymore . . . No. Of course, a bigger flowerpot, that's what I was telling you. What? No, I am not running off. Of course, love, I can get closer . . . tell me . . . What? Are you threatening me? What do you mean I'm not understanding your problem . . . of space? That's what I'm saying. No! Don't shout at me, darling, I have my device turned on.

Now what, my love? But all of you? . . . On the floor? How? Yes, my sweetie, but you see the problem is that the earth is under the floor . . . What do you mean, lift? The floor? You want me to lift the floor so I can bury you? Forgive me for laughing, my love, but it seems to me like "the cherry on top." But why would you want me to tear up the floor of my house? What do you mean, it's not my house? What do you mean, you were here before me? What's that smell? Love, what's that smell?

OK, then, let's get the job done. But I don't know if I can do it alone. Who? Joselino? Yes, yes, the boy who comes and helps me take care of you. But he doesn't get here until later.

What . . . ? A pen and a piece of paper? Of course, I must have a pen and paper, my love.

Who? Me? Of course, I know how to write, my love. Don't call me any more names, please.

OK, who is going to tell me what to write first?

What? What a beautiful image, that image seems so biblical to me . . . What? OK, I'll shut up.

Joselino

Audio: "Joselino! Joselino!" I heard someone say, barely, like a . . . when . . . I was just coming in the house and there was the mam' calling "Joselino! Joselino!" Her voice was worn out, she had but a hint of voice, who knows how long, how long she was there with the . . . crying out? . . . You can feel it when words get tired.

The lady was like . . . how can I explain, she was like, because she stayed, literally . . . how can I say . . . literally the lady was . . . planted. She had her legs buried in the ground, like this, up to the height of her thigh, more or less. She was buried like . . . right there in the earth, sir! She had raised all the floorboards like . . . she had taken all the plants of the house, and I am talking about a huge number of plants, sir!

I remember that in the room inside she had taken out the whole floor and had buried them in the ground below. She had taken them out of all their pots, which were *pff*! There was a tower of flowerpots, in a corner. I remember clearly that I thought the plants had kind of rebelled against the pots. You see, flowerpots were an invention of humans to do what they will, and move . . . how could I say . . . the immovable, you see; there's a reason plants grow roots, you know.

It couldn't fit inside my mind . . . how on Earth had the lady raised the floor alone? She was more than eighty years old.

She had all her clothes, like, they were broken, they were ripped. She had . . . all of her parts exposed. It made me nervous because I was a kid, and at that time she was like . . . like my mother. I went over and I wanted to take her like . . . She had her hands, where there was . . . in order to pull the . . . she had her hands with her fingernails pulled back because of all the force she had . . . Her knees were all scratched, and when the firemen came and they had to uproot her, you could even see the bones, because, you see, she had very thin skin.

Her hair was all tangled. She cried, she looked like . . . She cried like a little animal; the lady cried.

Me, I never went back to that house . . . I don't dare to pass by. It scares me. It's just . . . you can feel something there. The property is still there. The house is there, but no one ever pimped it. The plants ate up the house, it's all covered up. The vines covered the doors, you can't enter or leave anymore. The house is barely visible. The thing looks like the Garden of Eden, that thing ... It's been over twenty years already. That day, the lady said to me in a voice like a whisper: "Joselino, they say they want to reclaim the territory." I remember clearly that she asked me to take a wrinkled piece of paper she had in her hand, stained with blood. A letter, what do I know, that I later took for a poem ... well, I took that paper, and I saved it.

When I heard about the accident of this kid with the tree—the fireman that crashed with his bike and everything, against the tree ... ironic, right? Having been in so many fires, saving so many trees, to end up crashing into one—look, I know I have nothing to do with all of this, but I wanted to bring the paper because I think it can be of use to you. You are interrogating the wrong people, sir. Look, officer, you could see this coming, but this is such a slow coming that you don't see it, do you understand me? They are up to something. Maybe in five hundred years the world will be nothing but a green ball, pure vegetation, just like the lady's house, like the Garden of Eden ... do you understand me?

It's written in the poem left by the lady, I brought the paper so you can understand.

Well ... this wasn't the piece of paper, this is like going back in the lifetime of the paper, but I'll read it to you anyway, and we go back in time.

Manuel

Forgive me. Forgive me. Good heavens, forgive me. Stubborn are the times in which I try to make do with this. Injured I am, by the times in which I open my eyes to find this landscape. I am an animal. I am novice in the practice of inhabiting, novice in surviving. Thou wert all here before I was, nevertheless, it is me who survives with limited understanding, guilty reverse of a mystery, that you understand, however, better than I do. Because you live within time, not against it.

I am animal. My response to the world was to flee, my condemnation, then, was movement. When you stay, I move forward. Where you settle, I evade. In the face of difficulty, I avoid. Where you establish, I invade. I am animal. I hold my head with my two hands because in it wallows the question I ask of myself. Because my will is distributed in the absurd hierarchy of animal anatomy, in which the brain makes decisions for the hands, for the legs, for the kidneys.

Oh, noble vegetal dispersion! Noble and marvelous branched democracy. God, I beg of you: absolve me of the animal kingdom's forms! Give me something of theirs! May my lungs beat instead. May the tips of my fingers breathe, may my stomach think! May I feed with my skin, so that eating is more like touching than devouring. May the ever-changing forms of my body be my only language, so I become incapable of lying. May death be something that occurs in my chest, while my back, in turn, is born, so I never get the absurd idea that we are moving forward. May the passage of time be nothing more than a new ring in my trunk, every memory a layer of bark that covers me, so that I may touch my rugged memory.

Teach me this day, here, now, with what is left of you and what is left of me, how to speak in chemicals. Open for me your chemical recitation. Teach me how to speak in combinations of bromine and water, rather than in highs and lows. I want to use signifiers that taste of iodine. Signs that can only be deciphered with touch. Sentences that, if exposed to the sun, refract into mineral spectrums of blues and greens. I want to deliver speeches of poison. Let us recite poems whose lines only rhyme their levels of acidity.

What would it be like to grow without returning to the center, without ever regrouping, always moving outward? Never being able to close oneself upon oneself, never reaching the full circle of "This is I." To be, to grow, always, further out. So that that thing called I is only the memory of a seed. To be oneself, to be just oneself, is only a seasonal event. They tried to tell us all this, to cover the whole world with their varied words, but all they managed to say was: Leaf. Always the same leaf. It's not possible to escape planthood by means of plants. Nor to escape humanity by human means.

I am the last animal. Sitting at the site of the final catastrophe.

This forest was hell, ladies and gentlemen, even before the flames. This forest was made up only of pine trees. Imagine a city made up only of shoemakers. Only bakers, only nurses. All the pine trees planted in this forest were the same age—because this is how humans found it more efficient to plant. Imagine, if you will, a city only of children. Children alone. Here, ladies and gentlemen, it's as if a kindergarten had been burned down. "The wind is blowing, the wind is blowing hard, Mum!" The wind sounds of beauty in the forest until there's a spark. Until the earth dries up so much that he who softly whistled his friction with the vertices of the leaves suddenly no longer whistles but screams in a voice that is not his own but the voice of fire.

There are not four elements, there are three: water, air, and earth. Fire is not an element. Fire is a force that transforms one element into another. It transforms water into steam and wood into ash. By way of fire, we can all become other.

Hear me, Zeus: I know we can be other. How much other can we be? Must we burn to come to see? To God, I ask: Is there something in me that could become them? Given the green in my eyes perhaps? Or if, when I speak, I always use the same words, as if the words themselves were leaves, citations of other leaves, my words like foliage of alternate repetitions, perhaps?

And if those words were only flavors? Not an accumulation of signs that represent ideas . . . And if memory, then, was only body that is added onto body and not a series of images that represent events . . . We could then argue: No more representation! May nothing represent anything. May no one speak on behalf of anyone.

The hand thinks for itself, breathes for itself. Every limb has its own brain, its own lungs, its own eyes, its own ambitions, its own deities. Autonomy. The hand is not represented by ideas of the brain, nor by the needs of the eyes. No! It is only from political animal physiologies that tyrants could arise, or representative democracy, which is the same. Let us no longer continue down the immature route of the animal.

May the world once more become one big green ball. A sovereign vegetal state. Make landscape painters of those who in some near future wish to paint it.

I am the last animal. Come. Let me do what animals do and what plants do not: let me die.

Plants applaud. They ask for another one.

"Oh, no, we won't go! One more, one more!"

The girl takes a bow. Takes off the fireman suit and is now dressed as a tree. Ballet.

Girl: When you shed a leaf, how do you stop yourself from crying?

When it rains, how do you manage not to stick your tongue out?

When the sun is burning, how do you manage not to move?

Raúl: When you're changing your position, how do manage so that no one sees it?

Eva: When I ask you questions, how do you manage not to answer? When are you going to answer? Something?

Nora: Sweeties, do you remember the names you gave to your children this year?

Joselino: How many children did you have this year? And how many did you lose?

Eva: Because you know that we are made of flesh and that we eat meat? Would you like to try a salad?

Girl: Where is your heart?

Raúl: If we were to sing the national anthem now, where would you put your hand?

Girl: And where is your brain?

Raúl: If we were to decapitate you now, where would we cut?

Nora: Because, sweeties, you know that for us, everything that lives eventually has to die?

Mother: But if you never die, then how can we say you're alive?

—**They failed to identify any culprits.**
—What do you mean, there are no culprits?
—**The judge, the judges determined that no one is guilty . . .**
—No one is guilty?
—**Ma'am . . . please . . .**
—They can't just tell me no one is guilty . . .
—**He crashed against a tree . . .**
—But, how about the people that made the bike . . . huh?
—**The bike was working perfectly.**
—And the people from the municipality? Those in charge of . . .
—**They're not guilty.**
—Why so much moving here and there?
—**Work is like that these days, ma'am.**
—Work is like that?
—**Things are a little bit everywhere . . .**
—No, everything has its place.
—**Yes, but humans beings, I mean, they can move to different places, and that's good . . .**
—Good? For whom?
—**I don't know, for their careers . . .**
—Which career, the race against the tree? Do you know why the tree could have killed Manuel and not Manuel the tree? . . . Because the tree was still! It's that simple! Because it knew its place and it didn't move from its place. The stiller something is, the more it survives.
—**You have to sign the resolution, ma'am, you can do it anytime . . .**
—It will take me two thousand years to sign that resolution.
—**Whenever you want.**
—I'm going to sign it with my branches.
—**Sign it with whatever you want.**
—But do you understand that I now have a son in a . . . in a vegetative state?
—**Yes.**

—And what do I do with a son in a vegetative state? Do I water him?! What do I do? If he can't move, he can't move. How does something that can't move live? The tree is the culprit.
—**Yes.**
—It cut the power off, and in that moment, my son became a vegetable.
—**Yes.**
—The tree brought him to his kingdom.
—**Yes.**
—In that moment, in the dark, they took my son away to another kingdom. That's what they're plotting. Someone has to stand in the other's shoes. I understand.

July 2017

Acknowledgments

I am very thankful to Manuela Infante for her support and her involvement in this project, granting access to the photographic archive of *Estado Vegetal* and kindly collaborating on the authorial selection for this volume. Many thanks to all the contributors who invested time and thought into this collaborative effort. You have expanded my appreciation of *Estado Vegetal* and mapped new territory in the field of critical plant studies. Thank you for your determination, dedication, and kindness along the way. I am also particularly thankful to Caroline Picard (coeditor of the Art after Nature book series), Pieter Martin, Anne Carter, and everyone at the University of Minnesota Press for their support.

Contributors

Giovanni Aloi is associate professor, adjunct, of art history, theory, and criticism at the School of the Art Institute of Chicago. He is founder and editor in chief of *Antennae: The Journal of Nature in Visual Culture* and U.S. correspondent for *Esse Magazine—Art + Opinion.* He has authored four books, including *Why Look at Plants? The Vegetal World in Contemporary Art* and *Lucian Freud Herbarium.* He lectures at museums and universities internationally and is coeditor of the Art after Nature series at the University of Minnesota Press.

Maaike Bleeker is professor of theatre studies in the Department of Media and Culture Studies at Utrecht University. She is the author of *Visuality in the Theatre: The Locus of Looking.* She received a VENI research grant for her project "See Me, Feel Me, Think Me: The Body of Semiotics" and is coeditor of several volumes, including *Anatomy Live: Performance and the Operating Theatre, Performance and Phenomenology: Traditions and Transformations,* and *Transmission in Motion: The Technologizing of Dance.*

Lucy Cotter is a writer, curator, artist, and theorist. She has curated exhibitions and performances at Stedelijk Museum, Amsterdam; EYE Film Museum, Amsterdam; Kunstinstituut Melly, Rotterdam; Oregon Center for Contemporary Art, Portland; and The Kitchen, New York. She is author-editor of *Reclaiming Artistic Research* and publishes art criticism, theory, and fiction in the journals *Flash Art, Mousse, Artforum,* and *Third Text.* She presents lectures and workshops internationally.

Prudence Gibson is author of *The Plant Contract: Art's Return to Vegetal Life* and *Janet Laurence: The Pharmacy of Plants.* She scripts and produces video art, narrative projects, and curatorial approaches to plants inspired by new aesthetics and new plant science. She is lead CI on the ARC Linkage grant "Exploring the

Cultural Value of Sydney's Royal Botanic Gardens Herbarium Collection Using an Environmental Aesthetic."

Manuela Infante is a Chilean playwright, director, screenwriter, and musician who creates her own performances and tours in America, Europe, and Asia. Her works include *Estado Vegetal* and *Metamorphosis.*

Michael Marder is Ikerbasque Research Professor of Philosophy at the University of the Basque Country, UPV/EHU, Vitoria-Gasteiz. His books include *Grafts: Writing on Plants* (Minnesota, 2016), *Heidegger: Phenomenology, Ecology, Politics* (Minnesota, 2018), and *Green Mass: The Ecological Theology of St. Hildegard of Bingen.*

Dawn Sanders is associate professor in science and technology education at Gothenburg University. Her work focuses on inter-disciplinary approaches to "life as plant" and the materiality of gardens. Her research grants include the project "Beyond Plant Blindness: Seeing the Importance of Plants for a Sustainable World." She is the editor of "Standing in the Shadows of Plants: New Perspectives on Plant-Blindness," a special issue of *Plants, People, Planet.*

Catriona Sandilands is an environmental literary critic eco-cultural scholar and professor of environmental studies at York University. She is author of *The Good-Natured Feminist: Ecofeminism and the Quest for Democracy* (Minnesota, 1999) as well as more than eighty essays, reviews, journal articles, and chapters in edited collections. She is coeditor of *Queer Ecologies: Sex, Nature, Politics, Desire* and editor of *Rising Tides: Reflections for Climate Changing Times.*

Sibila Sotomayor Van Rysseghem is an actress, playwright, and director. She is a founder and member of colectivo LASTESIS, an artistic, feminist, and interdisciplinary group and creators of the performance *un violador en tu camino* (a rapist on your path), which has been performed in approximately forty countries. She is pursuing a PhD in social sciences at Universidad de Chile and works as a lecturer and researcher at Universidad de Valparaíso.

Mandy-Suzanne Wong is a Bermudian writer of fiction and essays. She is author of *Drafts of a Suicide Note*, a Foreword INDIES finalist, International Book Award finalist, and PEN Open Book Award nominee; *Listen, we all bleed*, an EcoLit Best Environmental Book of 2021 and a PEN/Galbraith nominee; *Animals across Discipline, Time, and Space*; *Awabi*, winner of the Digging Press Chapbook Series Award; and *The Box*.

Index

animal, ix, 2, 21, 42, 46, 52,
     55–56, 60, 71, 75, 81–82, 87,
     92, 115, 126, 128, 134–35,
     145–46, 152–55
Anthropocene, ix, 125
anthropocentrism, vii, 55, 88,
     134, 135
attunement, x, 111
audience, ix, 15, 16, 17, 18, 20–21,
     23–24, 28, 35, 38, 66, 67, 130,
     133, 124, 143

Barad, Karen, 8, 18, 15
Bataille, Georges, 31, 38, 39,
     40
biology, 69, 72, 73
body, 3, 8, 15, 35–36, 38, 69,
     71, 80, 92, 98, 100, 116, 128,
     131–32, 144, 153–54
botanical gardens, 47
botanical illustration, 52
Braidotti, Rosi, 8
branches, x, 3, 19, 34, 87–88, 90,
     97, 107–10, 114, 116–18, 121, 131,
     145, 156

climate change, xi, 66, 67
colonialism/postcolonialism,
     47, 88, 98, 102, 123

death, 7, 8, 10, 12, 59, 82, 88, 116,
     118, 108, 153
Deleuze, Gilles, 39, 42

Derrida, Jacques, 123
Duchamp, Marcel, 8

ecofeminism, 80, 85, 88, 91, 92
exotic, 47–48, 123
experimentalism, x, 29, 31, 32,
     33, 36–38, 84, 86, 136, 131,
     137

Fanon, Frantz, 8
forest, 28, 66, 71, 89, 90–91, 94,
     112, 114, 116, 121, 131, 141, 154
fungi, 70, 108, 112, 114, 132

Galliano, Monica, 8, 122
Guattari, Félix, 16–18, 39, 43, 51,
     52, 54, 123, 134–35

Hall, Matthew, 8
Haraway, Donna, 8, 67, 125
Hayles, N. Katherine, 8
houseplant, 46, 65, 72, 84, 121
humanism, 52, 100, 137
humanity, 4, 11, 66, 100, 153

Kimmerer, Robin Wall, viii, 51

leaves, x, 3, 49, 58, 70, 86–88,
     107–8, 116–18, 154, 109–10

Mancuso, Stefano, viii, 8, 9, 28,
     122, 126, 129, 132
Marder, Michael, viii, 16, 19, 28,

165

29, 32, 41, 39, 67, 91, 92, 121,
    122, 126
modernity, 3, 82
mythologies, 48, 51–53

networks, 70, 90–91, 98, 100,
    132
neurobiology, 29, 38, 30, 32, 42
nonhuman, viii, 16, 18, 20, 22,
    35, 48, 50, 51, 52, 53, 54, 56,
    59, 100, 122, 123, 124, 125, 129,
    130, 135, 137

otherness, ix, 19, 35–36, 59, 52,
    69, 74, 99, 125, 126, 128

plant-being, 134
planthood, 28, 32, 35, 40, 41, 153
plant movement, ix, 2, 5, 8, 11,
    15, 70, 72, 79–93, 152
plantness, v, 31, 65, 67, 69,
    71–77, 127
plant-thinking, ii, 10, 18, 19, 29,
    39, 129
polyphony, 32, 100, 117, 132
polyvocality, vii, 52, 56, 59, 132
posthumanism, viii, 8, 21, 100,
    104
potted plants, v, x, 45, 48, 50,
    54, 59, 60, 67, 81, 88, 92

representation, 15, 16, 18, 30, 35,
    39, 52, 53, 71, 99, 128, 154
roots, x, 7, 20, 27, 49, 59, 65, 70,
    85, 100, 110, 132

Salinas, Marcela, 2, 7, 10, 23, 28,
    33, 54, 70, 79, 139
science, 18, 60, 65, 70, 74, 85,
    121, 128, 129, 161, 162
sound, 21, 31, 36, 72, 79, 110, 118,
    122, 124, 144, 136
speculation, 5, 16, 18, 128, 133,
    130
Stein, Gertrude, 33
symbol, 47, 52, 65, 69, 73

tree, vii, ix, 3–4, 6, 9, 19–20, 25,
    27–29, 47, 49, 56, 65, 67, 71–72,
    76, 79, 80, 83–85, 87–89, 90,
    94–95, 107, 109–17, 130, 131,
    133, 139–40, 144, 146–49, 152,
    155, 157

unknowable, 27, 35, 36, 40

vegetality, 2, 92
vegetal time, vii, ix, 3, 8, 11, 12,
    23, 80–81, 86, 91
vegetarianism, 70–71
violence, 11, 56, 58, 94, 97, 100
voice, vii, 9, 10, 35–37, 52, 54, 56,
    67, 79, 85, 87–88, 98–99, 100,
    101, 110, 111, 132, 143, 154

weeds, 38, 72, 114, 115, 118
witnessing, 8, 10, 55, 70, 74, 84,
    90, 112, 142
Wynter, Sylvia, 8